D0208768

THE PEW WARMERS:
Thorns Among The Wheat

Gene Jackson

Copyright © 2008 by Gene Jackson

The Pew Warmers:
Thorns Among The Wheat
by Gene Jackson

Printed in the United States of America

ISBN 978-1-60477-607-2

All rights reserved solely by the author. The author guarantees all contents are original and do not infringe upon the legal rights of any other person or work. No part of this book may be reproduced in any form without the permission of the author. The views expressed in this book are not necessarily those of the publisher.

Unless otherwise indicated, Bible quotations are taken from the Holy Bible, New International Version (NIV) of the Bible. Copyright © 1973, 1978, 1984 by International Bible Society.

www.xulonpress.com

This book is dedicated to my wife, Dot, for her contributions of love, faithfulness, and patience.

Aspecial thanks of appreciation to Dr. Daphne O'Brien, North Carolina Wesleyan College, Rocky Mount, NC, for her editing and encouragement.

TABLE OF CONTENTS

INTRODUCTION

There is nothing wrong with Christianity! Churchgoers who have infiltrated the ranks of Christianity, who are without salvation, are trying to turn it into what it isn't. Today's churchgoing public knows very little about the Bible and its teaching. Multitudes are being misled into believing that churchgoing is the way to heaven.

Consider these statements as to their validity:

* Jesus drew the crowds who came out of curiosity, but only a few chose to follow Him.
* Multitudes claim to be followers of Christianity, but are without salvation.
* Seven out of every ten persons claiming Christianity are lost and without salvation, having never experienced repentance, faith, and salvation.
* Only one out of every four Christian churches in the United States has more born-again believers than those who have never been saved.
* Tens of millions on church rolls don't realize that they are lost.
* Multitudes of church members believe that churchgoing and good works are the doors to heaven.

* A vast number of ministers water down the teachings of Christ in their quest for members, financial rewards, and job security.
* More and more churches are relying on programs, instead of Christ, to attract numbers.
* Television evangelists and motivational speakers teach their audiences not about Christ, but how to become happy and rich while putting money into their own pockets.
* The media's reporting of Christianity is critical, negative, and adheres to opinionated ideas from so-called experts.
* Churches with large memberships and huge facilities believe that bigger is better, and much of their theology is more in tune with the lifestyles of attendees.
* A vast number of the churchgoing public attends church for the wrong reasons.
* Cash registers ring in Hollywood as speculative writers attempt to disprove the Bible.
* A vast number of churchgoers follow denominational doctrines instead of the Bible.
* Multitudes of the churchgoing public follow parental teachings instead of the Bible.
* Many churches rely on secular ways in attracting and keeping members.
* A backslidden condition is often used as an excuse to explain one's actions.

Backsliding is a fallacy and is not supported by Scripture.

* Churches don't make Christians. Only God can do that.
* Only God's Holy Spirit can draw a person to Jesus. It isn't the church.

The contents of this book are the results of decades of observing how churchgoing people live their lives; about their beliefs; and how multitudes are being led into believing that they are Christians. These writings are about what is being preached and practiced today in the name of Christianity.

What is being practiced and preached in most churches is labeled as Christianity, but is more akin to a social gospel attuned to the cultural lifestyles of the membership. Churchgoing or church membership is not the door that leads to eternal life and heaven. Neither is living a moral life or merely believing in God a doorway to a heavenly home. Biblical teachings indicate "only a remnant" will be saved and Jesus' teaching that "only a few" will find salvation, support these conclusions.

Some churchgoers who make claims to being Christians often adapt lifestyles which breed legalism. There are others who profess the name of Jesus and follow a lifestyle of licentiousness, while others practice lifestyles of complete freedom, doing anything that they think will make them feel good.

The Bible speaks of only one kind of Christian lifestyle. It is the one taught by Jesus Christ some two thousand years ago: repentance, which is a turning away from old ways and a turning back in faith to God. A noticeable change is to take place in the lifestyles of born-again believers upon their acceptance of Jesus, according to Paul, the apostle.

Nowhere do I claim to be a scholar or theologian, and neither am I a judge of human behavior. As a hole in a piece of dough is removed to make a doughnut, the teachings of the Bible have been removed from many churches, denominations, religious bodies, and within the home. Christianity, in its totality, is about Jesus, the Christ. Jesus Christ is Christianity, and without Christ there is no Christianity. This excludes Jehovah's Witnesses and Mormons, or Latter-Day Saints, from the ranks of Christianity.

It is often asked about children that have good parentage, but who go wrong: "who do they take that after?" The manner in which Christianity is being practiced and lived by the unsaved within churches leads the lost outside the church to ask the same question. The unsaved within the church are often misled into believing, by church leaders and ancestry, that they are following the teachings of Jesus. The lifestyles of today's churchgoing public will attest to the validity of the conclusions and opinions that will be expressed in these writings.

It is years of experience in observing, reading, and studying the lifestyles of churchgoing people, as well as what is taught and has been taught by religious leaders and parents for ages, that enables me to make the claim that there are far more unsaved persons in Christian churches today than there are those that are saved. I am not alone in these beliefs. Some theologians, scholars, and ministers will confirm these beliefs, and many will agree that today's Christianity is not the same as that taught by Jesus.

Many dedicated Christian pastors would like to rid their churches of the unsaved, but prefer not to face the consequences that would result from such actions. The majority prefer to maintain the status quo, and instead of trying to lead the lost to salvation, leave the future separation of the goats from the sheep up to God.

Attendance and membership in many churches are dwindling. Could it be that some unsaved churchgoers have grown tired of playing at Christianity? Worldly ways are brought into the church, and one gets the same things on the inside of the church that is being offered outside its walls. Therefore, why go to church?

My involvement with churches for over half a century substantiates the belief that the majority of churchgoers want only a "Sunday-morning type of religion." This "playing at Christianity" provides a turnoff for the unsaved or a non-

attending populace. Rubbing elbows with the churchgoing public, whether in or outside the walls of churches, exposes the unsaved to un-Christian like attitudes and lifestyles contrary to the teachings of Jesus.

It may come as a shock to some churchgoers who have been members of Christian churches for ages to discover that they are lost. Some know that they are tap-dancing around Christianity, while others are practicing what they have been taught from childhood.

It is disturbing that born-again believers are in the minority in the majority of the churches in America. It is not a denominational, sectional or regional thing. Infiltrators within Christian churches are dominant in seventy-five percent of Christian churches in every region of America with few exceptions.

No poll or survey can accurately prove or dispute these claims, because of the confusion among the masses over what Christianity really is. The lifestyles, beliefs, practices, and feelings held today by the unsaved churchgoing public are testimonies to the validity of these statements. The Bible becomes the Christian's source of truth.

This book is written for the purpose of having church-goers in every denomination examine their lives in light of the teaching of the Bible. Has there been a personal encounter with Jesus Christ or is it all about keeping up the tradition of churchgoing? Is Christianity being lived in terms of what is written in the printed pages of the Bible?

My prayer is that unsaved churchgoers on church rolls will discover that membership without salvation is as meaningless as the absent hole is in a doughnut. A doughnut, as we have been led to believe, is not a doughnut without the hole, and church membership without salvation from God is also as meaningless.

These pages are not written with the intent to be critical or judgmental or to be a condemnation of churchgoing people, churches, ministers or religious denominations. My hope, prayer, and purpose for these writings are for the multitudes of unsaved within Christian churches to discover the truth about Jesus Christ and be saved. It is about Jesus Christ, what the Bible teaches, and what His followers are to become.

CHAPTER ONE

JESUS, THE CHRIST

Christianity is all about Jesus Christ. It should be the quest of every church member to learn more than they already know about God's unique son and about the purpose for His coming to earth. It is essential for everyone to know who Jesus is—not who Jesus was.

Hundreds of years before Jesus walked along the shores of the river Jordan, many Old Testament prophets, at various intervals, prophesized of the Messiah that would come.

From the very first messianic prophecy in Genesis:... "And I will put enmity between you and the woman, and between your offspring and hers; he will crush your head, and you will strike his heel," until the end of Malachi, the coming of the Messiah (Jesus) was foretold.

Isaiah spoke about the coming of Jesus as a suffering servant. "Who has believed our message and to whom has the arm of the Lord been revealed?" Isaiah expounds on the sins of humanity and the suffering Messiah who "was oppressed and afflicted, yet he did not open his mouth; he was led like a lamb to the slaughter, and as a sheep before her shearers is silent, so he did not open his mouth."

Zechariah told of his coming when he wrote, "Rejoice greatly, O Daughter of Zion! Shout, Daughter of Jerusalem!

See, your king comes to you, righteous and having salvation, gentle and riding on a donkey, on a colt, the foal of a donkey."

Malachi foretold of a prophet similar to Elijah who would be the forerunner that would announce the arrival of Jesus, the Christ. "See, I will send you the prophet Elijah before that great and dreadful day of the Lord comes. He will turn the hearts of the fathers to their children, and the hearts of the children to their fathers; or else I will come and strike the land with a curse." Malachi was writing about John the Baptist, who over four hundred years later, would, upon seeing Jesus proclaim, "Look, the Lamb of God!"

Throughout the years from Moses until the last book of the Old Testament, the coming of the Messiah was foretold by many of the prophets. Only a few have been mentioned here. The religious leaders of Jesus' day had read, searched, and studied the scrolls of the prophets, and had been taught by their ancestors about the promised Messiah. But the religious people and political leaders of that day had one main problem: they wanted a Messiah contrary to the one that God sent.

The Messiah was to be a descendant of King David, and the religious leaders and the Jewish people expected Him to be an earthly king like David. Jesus didn't appear riding on a great white stallion with sword in hand to deliver the people from the oppression of the Roman army, but came the way that Zechariah foretold: riding on a donkey.

The purpose and destiny of the Messiah had been decided by God from before creation. The Messiah was destined to die on a cross for the sins of fallen humanity. Jesus' coming to earth as God wasn't an afterthought on the part of our Creator.

The virgin birth and the genealogies of Jesus are recorded in the gospels according to Matthew and Luke. New Testament writers made reference to the fulfillment of Old Testament prophecies in their acknowledgment that Jesus is the Messiah.

Very little is written or known about the earlier years of Jesus. Some thirty years after his birth, Jesus begins his ministry, appearing along the Jordan River asking to be baptized by John the Baptist. Jesus chose twelve men from varied backgrounds who would trudge around the countryside with their leader while he preached repentance by proclaiming: "the kingdom of heaven is at hand."

For the next three to three and one-half years, Jesus was constantly dogged, harassed, and hounded by the religious and political parties of his day. The Teachers of the Law, Pharisees, Sadducees, Herodians, Zealots, and Essenes were in conflict with the teaching of Jesus. Jesus took issue with these groups and was in conflict with their theology and political beliefs. Only a few within the parties of the Pharisees and Sadducees were willing to open their minds and hearts to Jesus' teachings.

These religious and political parties had their beliefs and traditions, and went about touting their own agendas. They remained embodied in the past by adding to and interpreting the teachings and traditions of Moses and their ancestors.

The religion of the Pharisees and the Sadducees had become a tradition of dos and don'ts. The Ten Commandments given by God to Moses had been dissected and dispersed into many facets, and in order to be holy, every "i" had to be dotted and every "t" had to be crossed. They had become slaves to the law.

To these parties, Jesus was only a carpenter's son walking around the countryside, saying and doing things, even miracles, in conflict with what they taught, believed, and held so dear. And what was tragic and went against their beliefs; was that this Jesus was doing some of them on the Sabbath day, when no work was to be done at all.

Jesus' ministry attracted the masses. Multitudes came to hear his teachings, to witness miracles, to see the healing of the sick, the raising of the dead, and to be in his presence. His ministry was causing some to ask: "Is this the Messiah?"

The religious and political groups were being put to the test. The people began to question the authority of these parties since the teachings of Jesus were conflicting with what these groups had been teaching and leading others to believe. Jesus made it clear that he had not come to change the law as given to Moses or to establish an earthly kingdom. "Do not think that I have come to abolish the Law or the Prophets, I have not come to abolish them but to fulfill them."

Jesus called these religious leaders hypocrites and vipers. These parties, seeing the mounting popularity of Jesus, began to apply more and more pressure by asking trap-setting questions and seeking ways to arrest him. People began to say that Jesus was a prophet, while others said that he was the Christ. Some said that he was from Satan and wanted him arrested, but were afraid of the popularity of Jesus with the people.

The Pharisees and Sadducees, in order to cope with this increasing popularity on the part of Jesus, began to look for ways to arrest him. Jesus, knowing that his earthly ministry was not over, began to avoid places where he might be arrested. Those that were being healed by Jesus were told not to tell anyone who it was that had made them well.

Jesus, on one occasion, asked his disciples: "Who do people say the Son of Man is?"

They replied by saying, "Some say John the Baptist; others say Elijah; and still others, Jeremiah or one of the prophets."

"But what about you?" he asked. "Who do you say I am?"

Simon Peter answered, "You are the Christ, the Son of the living God."

Hundreds of years before God came down to earth to become humanity, Isaiah, the prophet, said this about the Messiah: "For to us a child is born, to us a son is given, and the government will be on his shoulders. And he will be called Wonderful Counselor, Mighty God, Everlasting Father, Prince of Peace. Of the increase of his government and peace there will be no end. He will reign on David's throne and over his kingdom, establishing and upholding it with justice and righteousness from that time on and forever. The zeal of the Lord Almighty will accomplish this."

Jesus Christ, the Jewish Messiah, came to live and to die on this earth to save a fallen race from their sins. He was rejected by the multitudes, and only a few received him. He came to die for our sins in order that we might live by being born-again spiritually to God.

He conquered death's dominion over every believer, who by their faith, believe that he is God's Messiah. Jesus is the door through which a person has to enter to get to God. Believers are adopted as sons and daughters into His kingdom upon repentance and the confession of their faith in Him.

"Who crucified Jesus?" many have asked.

We, who have repented of our sins and received His grace, will say, "We did!"

And as John, the apostle, wrote: "But these are written that you may believe that Jesus is the Christ, the Son of God, and that by believing you may have life in His name."

CHAPTER TWO

A SELF-EXAMINATION

"... The disciples were called Christians first at Antioch." Acts 11:26.

BELIEVERS ARE CALLED CHRISTIANS

It is interesting to note that the followers of Jesus were first addressed, out of ridicule, as Christians in Antioch, a place where Jews and Gentiles, with nothing in common, were being saved. It was more than amazing to those witnessing the changes in lifestyles of those claiming Christianity, that not only Jews, but Greeks were professing Christ. Racial barriers were being destroyed, and drastic changes were taking place in the lives of those being saved by the grace of God. Those outside the circle of believers were noticing the effects of Christianity on those who had chosen to follow a resurrected Savior.

The Bible doesn't tell us how these converts during the first century reacted to the ridicule of following a Jew who had been crucified on a cross. Yet we know this ridicule didn't prevent them from attracting others to their faith. Barnabas, the encourager, upon discovering the saving faith of the people in Antioch, enlisted the Apostle Paul to come to Antioch to help in the teaching of these believers.

THE CROSS AS A SYMBOL OF CHRISTIANITY

People today casually hang crosses around their necks as adornments, but never follow or are taught about what it is to be a Christian. The adornments of today's crosses don't do anything in attracting others to Jesus Christ. These adornments, worn by today's society, become only ornaments of decoration, and the wearers, by their non-Christian lifestyles, betray not only themselves but the One whom they are openly endorsing to others.

I have moved throughout jails and prisons as a messenger of the Lord Jesus Christ and have found prisoners weaving crosses out of threads and giving them to their cellmates. Some prisoners are very talented and the crosses which they weave are sought out by others who want to wear them around their necks, but who have no saving intimate knowledge of Jesus and His sacrifice for their sins on the Cross. These weavers of crosses, because of inactivity within their cells, whether believers or not, don't explain to their cellmates or to others the significance of these crosses; therefore, the wearing of these crosses is without meaning or dedication.

I have found only a few self-professing Christians who are willing to talk openly about their faith and their salvation. Some have done it sheepishly and apologetically, blushing timidly when asked about their feelings about Jesus. This is not to say that those who react this way are not saved and are not Christians. Every person is a unique personality and reacts according to his or her own conditioning. It is not to be expected of or asked of a Christian to climb to the highest rooftop and to profess his or her faith in Jesus the Savior. Jesus says, "Whoever acknowledges me before men, I will also acknowledge him before my Father in heaven." These acknowledgments come in varied ways.

The Bible teaches the followers of Jesus Christ to live a lifestyle worthy of their faith. It teaches that we no longer belong to ourselves, but to the One who has now called us to a higher calling. Changes occur in a person's perspectives, goals, and no doubt their lifestyles upon repentance and faith in the Lord Jesus.

A SELF-EVAULATION

A measuring rod for determining whether one has been changed is to make a simple evaluation of one's lifestyles, values, and commitment to Jesus. Consider these questions, regardless of whether you are young or old, as if today were the last day of your earthly life.

YES OR NO?

Are you actually trying to overcome your temptations to sin?

- Are you willfully engaged in an extramarital relationship without feeling any remorse for your sinfulness?
- Are you engaging in sexual activities outside of marriage?
- Are you willfully engaging in sin and not doing anything about it?
- Are you unwilling to control your sinful desires?
- Are you unremorseful when you willfully commit sins?
- Are you profaning the name of God in your everyday speech?
- Are you enjoying dirty jokes when you hear them?

- Are you a teller of dirty jokes?
- Are you living one lifestyle on Sunday and another one during the week?
- Are you living a lifestyle that is different from those who are not claiming Christianity?
- Are you a participant in pornography?
- Are you living a lifestyle that would be an example of goodness to another?
- Are you interested in reading and studying the Word of God?
- Are you more interested in reaching personal goals than in seeking God's will?
- Are you trying to live by Biblical teachings or by your standards?
- Are you unforgiving of others?
- Are you racially motivated or do you despise others?
- Are you ignoring the sin in your life, feeling that God will forgive you when you ask?
- Are you comparing your lifestyle with the lifestyle of another?
- Are you living a lifestyle that is different from the one lived before your salvation or is there the absent of a transition from your old life to a new way of life?
- Are you more interested in expressing your needs while praying instead of praising God?
- Are you experiencing the presence of God in your everyday life?

Some will claim these questions have nothing to do with whether they are Christians or not. But the truth here is that God gives to believers the power to overcome their sinful passions from their previous desires and ways. The power within born-again believers is greater than the power that is in the world.

This line of questions should help in leading a person in determining his or her spiritual condition. Affirmative answers or explanations to any of these questions should bring conviction, remorsefulness, and recommitment to a Christian heart. It may also lead the unsaved to conviction, forgiveness, repentance, and faith in the Lord Jesus.

Would the writers of the Bible continue to disgrace the teachings of their Lord by living their lives contrary to His teachings? Those who engage in sinful activities that are contrary to Biblical teachings should examine their lives to determine if they are in the faith.

It's possible that you have never had a repentant-heart encounter with Jesus Christ, while all the time believing that you are a Christian, but having never been saved. A self-examination of lifestyles is to bring an awareness as to whether a person is living a life which glorifies God, and is Christian, or is one of total self-gratification. There is no possible way to serve two masters: God on Sunday and Satan during the week.

MEDITATION

A TRIP BACK IN TIME

My friend and I took a trip to Cana in Galilee. We wanted to visit the area where Jesus had performed his first miracle, so we tried to find the location of the wedding banquet to which Jesus and his disciples had been invited.

According to the customs of that day and time, a wedding was a very happy occasion—sometimes lasting for a week. Town-folks from all around were invited to the festivities, sometimes even the entire town. It wasn't a difficult task for us to find the location, especially since Jesus had been there only a few days before. Some would never forget the things said about him and what he had done while there.

Our intent for coming here was to speak with the master of the banquet, for he would know more about the banquet, and what had taken place, than any of the others. We had for him some questions about the events that had taken place at the wedding.

Why would Jesus turn water into wine that could cause people to get drunk, perhaps causing some to do unholy things? Why didn't Jesus do something different, this having been His very first miracle.

Some people back home in America wanted to know if the wine was fermented and would cause drunkenness. A lot of questions were being raised about this miracle, because many teetotalers in today's churches are strictly against the consumption of any type of alcohol. In today's society, many drink to get drunk, while thinking the drunker they become, the more fun they are going to have.

We were soon following directions from those that we had asked about where to find the master at the banquet that Jesus had attended. These directions led us to a Jewish merchant, a well-known planner and caterer who had a shop in the downtown area of Cana.

As we entered the shop, a diminutive man with fat cheeks and a protruding stomach, fit for any Santa Claus suit, greeted us with a most jolly welcome that expressed a hope for entrepreneurial gain.

"Greetings," he said. "How may I help you?"

"We have been told that you were in charge of the wedding that Jesus and his disciples, as well as his mother, attended not too long ago."

"Oh, yes!" he exclaimed with glee. "It was a wonderful wedding! Everything went so well. The bride and groom made wonderful provisions for their guests. In fact, almost everyone in town was there."

"We understand that Jesus turned some water into wine, and we wanted to know if it was truly fermented, and what affect the miracle had on the guests?"

"I thought that the groom was so clever, he said, because of the way that he did things. We thought that we had run out of wine, and before I knew what others were saying about it, my assistants brought me six ceremonial cleaning jars filled to the brim with a wine that was better than anything that I have every tasted. In fact, I told the groom that he had outdone himself—disguising the wine by putting it into water jars, and keeping the best to last.

"But we understood that the wedding banquet had run out of wine, and that Jesus, being encouraged by his mother to help out the bride and groom, turned plain old water into wine."

"From what I have heard about Jesus, said the shop owner, he could have done it without blinking an eye. Some told me later that Jesus had done it. However, I was so busy doing the job that I was entrusted with, that I failed to notice. If he did, he surely made my job a lot easier. This I can attest to: you don't find or buy wine of that quality from anyplace that I know about."

"But, what about Jesus?" we asked. "What was it like for you to be in the same place as Jesus, and for you to be catering an affair where not only Jesus was present, but Jesus' mother, plus his disciples?"

"You don't listen too well!" said the shop owner with a smile. "I've told you that I was up to my neck in trying to keep everyone happy. I was too busy to notice what was taking place."

We thanked the shop owner for his willingness to talk with us for a few moments, closing the door behind us as we left his premises.

I stopped outside the little shop, turned to my friend, and said: "Surely God was at the banquet, and the master of the banquet knew it not!"

"Yes," he replied. "We miss the miracles by becoming too busy with the material things surrounding us."

—derived from John 2:1-11.

CHAPTER THREE

THE STRUGGLE WITHIN CHRISTIANS

Within every born-again believer there is an ongoing struggle to do evil instead of becoming the "workshop of good works" that God called us to. When there is no struggle in the life of a Christian, there is no salvation.

Churchgoing is an attempt by the lost, not only to get to heaven but to appear good to others. For the saved, churchgoing is to honor, glorify, worship, and praise God. God is to be number One in the life of a born-again believer. The Christian leaves the church grounds to be of service to others, make disciples, be a witness, and to live a life that will honor and glorify God.

The apostle Paul, after his salvation, struggled with an effort to do good instead of doing or being evil. Paul writes: "So I find this law at work: When I want to do good, evil is right there with me. For in my inner being I delight in God's law; but I see another law at work in the members of my body, waging war against the law of my mind and making me a prisoner of the law of sin at work within my members. What a wretched man I am! Who will rescue me from this body of death? Thanks be to God—through Jesus Christ our Lord!"

THE HOLY SPIRIT WITHIN THE CHRISTIAN

The person who has been saved by the grace of God has a Helper, the Holy Spirit, living inside of him that gives the necessary strength and power to restrain from the forces of sin that will always be there in body and in mind. The apostle recognized that growth, power, and the will to overcome sin came only through Jesus Christ our Lord.

Christ Jesus died for our sins and ascended into heaven so that the promised Helper could now live inside of the born-again believer. Jesus not only becomes Savior to the born-again believer but he becomes the believer's Lord. The power to resist evil is available only to the born-again believer. The indwelling Spirit of God is absent from the life of the lost.

Churchgoers who are unsaved feel no remorse when sinning, often making the claim that they are only human. The continuation of sin in their lives is merely acknowledged as a condition that they have no control over. Therefore, there is no effort on their part to conquer or overcome the temptations which they are experiencing.

There is no remorse on the part of the unsaved, only a feeling of guilt and the belief that because of their humanity, they are powerless to do anything about it. Unbelievers blame their sins on their humanity, and so do some born-again believers. Believers have the Holy Spirit; unbelievers do not.

The excuse often used by unbelievers is that because of having been born with a sinful nature, it is only natural for one to submit to sinful ways and to live in sin. This is the excuse used primarily by many who claim the name of Christianity.

There is no struggle within the life of the unsaved in their effort to be good instead of evil. As the saying goes: "no pain, no gain," or it could be: "no struggle with temptations, no salvation."

The unbelievers' guilt for their sin is not toward God, but toward the people who are being wronged by their sins. When a husband or wife is living in adultery, they feel guilty about their mate and children and what infidelity is doing or will do to them or their marriage. Their greatest fear is not of God and his wrath upon sin, but of being exposed to those who trust and have put their faith in them. Today's surveys show that over twenty percent of husbands and wives are now living in adulterous relationships. Many of them will claim to be Christians.

Born-again believers, like the apostle Paul, are torn between doing evil and doing good. We are humans and blame our humanity when we sin. Christians need to be reminded that Jesus was also human, but without sin.

The saved should be aware that they have become God's workshop and should know that they have been saved to live their lives for Jesus. Their spirit will bear witness with the Holy Spirit living within them that they are now the children of God.

TEMPTATIONS BY THE DEVIL

Often I am asked by some who are claiming the name of Jesus to pray with them that they can overcome the temptations in their lives. Yet some of them have never yielded their lives to God. They are fully aware of what the temptations are that are causing them to do the evil that they are doing. Some of these requests for prayer are sincerely motivated by a desire to be good instead of evil, for it is the doing of evil that has brought them to their need of prayer.

What temptations are for some may not be temptations for others. The devil is aware of our weaknesses, and appears to all of us in different disguises. When the devil appeared to Jesus in the wilderness, he knew that Jesus had been fasting for a long period of time, and that he was hungry. The devil said to Jesus, ". . . tell these stones to become bread." Jesus was in total trust with God and used the Scriptures to refute the devil and his temptations.

Jesus' instructions to his disciples were to lead prayerful lives, asking God to "Lead us not into temptation, but deliver us from the evil one." The devil is the one that is leading the temptations, and God is in allowance because of our free will to choose right or wrong.

The apostle Paul, writing to the church at Corinth says, "So, if you think you are standing firm, be careful that you don't fall! No temptation has seized you except what is common to man. And God is faithful; he will not let you be tempted beyond what you can bear. But when you are tempted, he will also provide a way out so that you can stand up under it."

Within the Christian or born-again believer there will always be a struggle between good and evil. This is not true for the unsaved, since the devil already has the unsaved under his control. The devil is there to tempt the Christian at every turn of the road, and sometimes roads are taken that lead into sinful acts. Hands touch often the stove to see if it is hot or we look enticingly at things around us that will lead us to stray from the One that we profess to love with all our heart, soul, and strength. When we enter into sin, there is no one to blame it on but ourselves. The devil didn't make us do it or anyone else for that matter. He will always throw obstacles in our paths.

Churchgoers are reminiscent of seagulls flying in precise formation along the shores of an ocean. In the beginning, they fly in unity as they follow the leader. One by one they begin to peel off and to take another course. So it is with believers and non-believers as they gather together in the pews. They sit, sing, and stand together, but upon leaving the sanctuary, the majority peel off one by one to follow their own instincts.

MEDITATION

A TRIP BACK IN TIME

My friend and I came upon a farmer preparing his farm field for planting. The farmer engaged us in conversation, having this to say:

"Are you looking for the spot where Jesus sat while he was teaching?" he asked. "This has become a very popular route for strangers to take since Jesus and his disciples, along with some followers, were by here the other day. They sat down over there and Jesus began to teach them. In fact, if strangers like you continue coming to this area, I might make me some extra money by conducting a few tours of my farm fields."

"Did you get close enough to the group to hear what Jesus was teaching?" we asked.

"Yes," he answered. "Jesus, perhaps seeing one of my freshly planted fields from the day before, began to talk to them about different types of soil."

"I had heard about Jesus before he came this way, and it was rumored that he was a carpenter. But, if you had heard him talking to that group, you would have thought that he had been farming all of his adult life. He knew all about farming and what farmers encounter in making ends meet out here in these fields. As I listened to him, it seemed as if he was empathizing with my plight as a farmer, and that he was talking directly to me. He certainly got my attention!"

"As I prepare these fields for planting," he continued, "I encounter soil so hardened that it becomes difficult to plow. Then there's the soil that is very rocky, the sandy soil, and of course, the soil that is darkened with richness. Jesus was talking about these same types of soils."

"As a farmer, you see, I get my sack of seeds, throw them over my shoulder, and walk all across these fields, broad-casting my seeds in all these types of soil, hoping that this might be the year when every bit of ground in that field will produce a harvest better than last year. But, I always know where to look in my field for the harvest that is going to be the best. Jesus knew all about what he was teaching."

The farmer was about to continue with his dialogue, but my friend interrupted him.

"What exactly was Jesus saying?" asked my friend.

The farmer began by saying: "Jesus said that a farmer was scattering his seed. Some fell along a path, and that birds came and ate it up. Some fell, he said, on rocky places, where there was not much soil, and because of shallow soil, the plants could not stand the heat of the sun and soon died, having no roots. Then Jesus told about the seeds that fell among thorns, and how the weeds choked out the plants. Then he said that the seeds sowed in the good soil would multiply sometimes as much as thirty, sixty, or even a hundred times."

"Was Jesus right about the four types of soils in your fields?" my friend asked.

"He was perfectly right," said the farmer.

"But Jesus was a religious man," we added. "What can different types of soil have to do with people?"

"You know," he said, "I was so enthralled by what Jesus was saying about farming that I never made that connec-tion. All the time that I was in the presence of Jesus, I felt some warmness within me that had been missing before, but I couldn't get my mind off of farming."

Before saying our goodbyes to the farmer, he asked our opinion about charging those that would come out of curiosity to his farm fields, knowing that Jesus had once come that way.

"Is there money to be made in such a venture?" the farmer asked.

Trying to avoid a direct answer to his question, we gazed across his farm fields and said:

"We would have previously rewarded you to distinguish for us the differences in the soil in your fields, but having been here to walk where Jesus walked, and believing that the soil relates to people, there is no further need for us to look at the soil."

Leaving the farmer alongside his field, my friend turned to me and asked: "Considering the four types of soil as the way that we as people respond to the message of God, which type of soil do you think is typical of our farmer friend?"

—derived from Mark 4:1-20.

CHAPTER FOUR

WANDERERS IN THE WILDERNESS

In reply (to Nicodemus) Jesus declared, "I tell you the truth, no one can see the kingdom of God unless he is born again." John 3:3

I would be the first to agree that people take passages from the Bible out of context, and by twisting them, support their position on certain matters. This is often done by those who are attempting to support a specific belief. Those who are opposed to views held by others seek passages in defense. Our Counselor and Guide in such matters is God's Holy Spirit, because He doesn't give conflicting messages. My conclusions about the majority of the churchgoing public being without salvation are centered on the overall teachings of the Bible, and not on passages taken out of context.

Throughout these pages, my writings focus on the teachings of Jesus, comparing them with the beliefs of today's churchgoing public who claim to be following His teachings. The Christianity that is being practiced and lived today by the majority of churchgoers is a distant cry from what Jesus taught when he invited the lost to God.

BY THEIR ACTIONS YOU WILL KNOW THE UNSAVED

The conclusions that I draw about the practices and beliefs of those who are lost and who are infiltrating Christianity today, regardless of denominations, are as follows:

* Many church members know about the Cross, but don't know the Person of the Cross.
* Many church members reared in the church have never considered themselves as sinners.
* Many have never had a "repentance and faith" encounter with the Son of God.
* Many have an intellectual knowledge of Jesus, but lack the heart-felt encounter.
* Many trust in a "feeling," but lack a "need-felt fulfillment."
* Many trust in what they have been taught and led to believe by others.
* Many consider the United States to be a Christian nation, entitling them to be called Christians.
* Many believe that if they were reared in a Christian home, they are going to heaven.
* Many believe that if their parents were Christians, they too are Christians.
* Many believe that if they have been christened, confirmed, or circumcised they will go to heaven.
* Many know very little about the teachings of the Bible and what it is to be saved.
* Many believe that if they have been baptized, they have been saved.
* Many believe that if they partake of Holy Communion, they are saved.
* Many believe that if they live a good life, they are going to heaven.

* Many believe that if they do good deeds and are moral, they will go to Heaven.
* Many believe that churchgoing is the gateway to heaven.
* Many compare their lifestyles with the less favorable lifestyles of others.
* Many believe that the prerequisite to heaven is a belief in God.
* Many believe that there is no hell, but only a heaven.
* Many are "hoping" that they get to Heaven.
* Many attend church out of a superstitious nature.
* Many attend church because it gives them a "good and respectable" feeling.
* Many attend church for personal and social reasons.

ONLY ONE ROAD LEADS TO HEAVEN

There is total confusion among churchgoers about Christianity's teachings. This is partly attributable to denominational teachings about doctrines which are secondary and not about the teachings of the One who died on the Cross. It is also in the failure of the churchgoing public to read and study the Bible. Why else would there be so many split-offs and religious bodies teaching doctrines contrary to the truths of the Bible? A denominational church on every corner of a town testifies to the fact that Christianity has become a cafeteria-style religion.

Katharine Jefferts Schori, present bishop-elect of the Episcopal Church, says that "she personally believes in a relationship with God through Jesus, but does not see it as the only true path. If we insist we know the one way to God, we're putting God in a very small box." This is the "beliefs and feelings held by the leader of a 2.3-million member denomination which is the American branch of the Anglican family. Seven U.S. dioceses have rejected her authority and asked the Archbishop of Canterbury, Rowan Williams, the Anglican spiritual leader, to assign them another national leader.

Many who are not knowledgeable of Biblical teachings will be led astray by her personal view of Jesus and "being not the only true path." The teachings of Jesus have been changed throughout the centuries by religious leaders and denominations to suit the philosophy of the masses. Eventually, these personal beliefs are handed down from generation to generation.

Jesus made a promise that when he went to be with God the Father, he would send the Holy Spirit to each believer as a Counselor or Comforter. The Holy Spirit is not going to be contradictory in his teaching to believers—teaching one believer something that is different than what He teaches another.

The Holy Spirit is grieved when our will is contrary to the will of God. He convicts believers of their wrongness when failing to act as children of God. Nevertheless, there are religious leaders who will continue to cater to the wishes of their hearers or who will disperse their beliefs to others.

THE NARROW GATE THAT LEADS TO HEAVEN

Jesus says, "Enter through the narrow gate. For wide is the gate and broad is the road that leads to destruction, and many enter through it. But small is the gate and narrow the road that leads to life and only a few find it." This passage supports the claim that there are more unsaved within the church than those who are saved and who are true believers. With 2.3 billion persons throughout the world claiming Christianity, today's secularism wouldn't be as godless, if Christ were in hearts instead of words. It would be more understandable to believe that these masses are "leaning" toward Christianity than to say that they are born-again believers.

I have watched football stadiums filled to capacity with self-proclaiming Christians who scream their lungs out over plays, tackles, and touchdowns. Has today's world ever seen that much excitement over the cause of Christ and the salvation of sinners? That kind of enthusiasm is absent from today's churchgoing crowds that attend only when they are in the mood.

TEACHINGS WITH ONLY ONE ANSWER

Learning institutions require students to be tested to see if they qualify to go to the next level. Consider a question such as this: To get to heaven a person must: (1) read the Bible (2) go to church (3) give money to the church (4) be baptized (5) live a good life, and (6) be a church member. The option is given to circle as an answer, (a) all of the above; (b) one of the above; or (c) none of the above. Some will answer with "all of the above" and many will choose "one of the above," instead of the correct answer of "none of the above."

An unsolicited email came my way a few days ago with the following:

"The teacher in a Sunday school class of small children tested the class to see if they understood the concept of getting to heaven. The class was asked by the teacher whether if she sold her house, had a gigantic garage sale, and gave all of the money to the church, she would get to heaven?" "No!" the children answered.

The teacher continued with the next question: "If I cleaned the church every day, and kept everything neat and tidy, would that get me to heaven?" Again the children answered: "No!" that wouldn't get their teacher to heaven.

By now the teacher was feeling proud of her teaching and her students, and began to smile.

"Well, then, if I was kind to animals, and gave candy to all the children, and loved my husband, would that get me to heaven?" The children again answered with a hearty, "No!"

By now the teacher was bursting with pride for them and she continued with the next question: "Well, then how can I get into Heaven?"

A five-year-old boy shouted out, "YOU GOTTA BE DEAD!"

DISCOVERING THE RIGHT ANSWER

Today's populace is of the opinion that there are many roads to heaven, and are not aware of the one that Jesus spoke about. The motivation of the earth's population is to get to heaven without having to change their lifestyles, by not having repentant hearts and forgiveness for their sins.

Unsaved infiltrators in the Christian faith are playing at church with motives contrary to those of Jesus as the Head of the Church. A prerequisite for membership in any church "should" be repentance for sins, and a faith leading to salvation in the death, burial, and resurrection of Jesus, the Christ. Seven out of every ten persons who claim membership in the majority of churches in America have not come by the way of the Cross, having had no personal encounter with Jesus. "It's the same old me," as the song goes.

Question any ten church members today and you will get several different answers about what their beliefs are pertaining to church membership; churchgoing; what Christianity is all about; and which roadmap they are following in reaching heaven. Many will tell you about their feelings—not about their faith, and all of them will tell you that they believe in God. The Scriptures say, "You believe that there is one God. Good! Even the demons believe that... and shudder." Feelings and unbiblical beliefs are not the doorways to salvation.

How great is this problem of infiltration of churches by the unsaved, and is it something that Christians and churches should be concerned with? The answer is an unequivocal "yes." The answer to this infiltration won't be found in building more facilities and growing larger churches. Neither will mega-churches and larger memberships solve the existing problem. Neither will motivational speakers preaching riches for everyone while they fill their pockets with cash lead their listeners to follow the One who died on the Cross. The Gospel of Jesus Christ has to be preached and the Bible taught to bring the unsaved to repentance.

The church as we know it today, regardless of denomination, is like a cruise ship loaded down with churchgoing passengers. The saved go to eat on the portside of the ship and the unsaved partake of their meal on the starboard side. The weight is so great on the starboard side of the ship that the ship begins to capsize. The saved and unsaved begin to run for the exits, but only exits on the portside of the ship are opened. Jesus is the only exit into heaven, for He says, "I am the way and the truth and the life. No one comes to the Father except through me."

Lost church members and a vast majority of churches are wandering in the wilderness. Their unbelief is similar to that of the Israelites that came out of Egypt, and because of their disobedience and unbelief were not permitted by God to enter into the land flowing with milk and honey. Will seventy percent of the churchgoing public continue to wander in the wilderness of their unbelief and never reach the promised land of heaven?

MEDITATION

A TRIP BACK IN TIME

"Care to take another trip with me?" I asked my friend.

"Where?" he asked.

"Back to Galilee," I answered. "Let's go and see Jesus."

"But, Jesus is not there," he replied. "He was crucified over two thousand years ago."

"He's there," I said. "Let's just go back in time."

We were soon knocking at the door of Peter's mother-in-law. Barely cracking open the door, with tired, sleepless eyes, she questioned our early morning knock.

"We would like to speak with Jesus," I said.

"You and so many others," she said. "Jesus, wanting to be alone, left early this morning for some hillside praying." With this said, she continued: "You should have been here last night, for the entire town was at our door to be near the man that healed my fever, cured others, and drove out demons from demon-possessed people."

"Will he be coming back to your house today?" we asked.

"Only our God in heaven knows the answer to that," she said. "Jesus only passes this way ever so often with my son-in-law, Peter. The best thing that has ever happened to Simon was when he, at Jesus' invitation, decided to follow and dedicate his life to Jesus. I didn't approve at first of him leaving behind my daughter for Jesus, but, according to Peter, that was the way it had to be. Jesus would have it no other way."

"Thank you for speaking with us about Jesus, but we will have to be going," I said. "We are sorry that we disturbed you at this early hour, and have missed seeing Jesus."

"So am I," she said. "So many people will miss seeing him, and I do wish that you had come earlier. So many, like you, have waited too late to come to Jesus, and will miss him altogether."

As we walked away, going back to our place in time, she called out to us:

"I'm sorry that I didn't ask your name, but it really doesn't matter. Simon Peter says that Jesus knows the name of every person. Simon says that Jesus will be the one seeking you."

—derived from Mark 1:29-39.

CHAPTER FIVE

A LITTLE YEAST

". . . But be on your guard against the yeast of the Pharisees and Sadducees." Matt. 16:11b

SECULARISM WITHIN CHURCHES

People go their doctors when they are sick and feeling pain. Often a shot or pain medication is given or prescribed. Sometimes all that is needed is to be told to take a couple of aspirin and rest for awhile. Within a matter of moments after getting shots or taking medication, the pain and sickness are relieved. However, that is not true of the yeast which infiltrates churches. Unbelievers attract more unbelievers until they grow to outnumber the saved. There is a remedy for this, yet only a few will realize the need for a cure.

It only takes a little yeast to leaven an entire congregation. The "yeast" infiltrating today's churches is the secularism of today's churchgoing public. Christians are to live in the world, but are not to adopt or comply with society's standards. The lifestyles of today's secular culture have become mighty rivers, flowing over the cliffs of Christian ethics and values. The church, being exposed to the yeast of the lost, comes down with a deadly virus... a virus of unbelievers.

The churchgoing public has become brain-damaged by television, the internet, magazines, celebrities, and consumerism. Today's churchgoers believe they have to accept and adapt to the same venue existing within the lives of friends, associates, and the folks next door in order to fit in.

Some churchgoers want what the church is trying to represent, so they bring their cultural standards into their local churches and, eventually, their standards become the dominant ones. After awhile, churches begin providing and offering the same programs existing in the secular realm, because that is what the churchgoing public expects. Unsaved churchgoers within churches soon implement within churches their programs to coincide with their secular pursuits.

The dress of the street has become today's norm for some churchgoing attendees, which is evident in the way that some clothe themselves. I am not suggesting that we go to church in our "Sunday's best," but primarily I am speaking of the flesh-revealing attire being worn within the walls of a sanctuary. Some attire is not respectful to the God that we are worshiping. Clothing fit for a worshipful occasion has become no more than the attire being worn when strolling down Bourbon Street on any given night.

It is perfectly fitting if attending a worship service on a beach to be attired in appropriate beach clothing. If worshiping in a rodeo arena, nothing is wrong about being clothed in western wear. The attire should be conducive to the atmosphere. You don't find people in rescue missions worshiping in business suits. Yet if the present clothing trend continues, within the next few years, clothing worn at church will not be distinguishable from that worn to a local gym, at an outdoor social event, or out on a jogging trail. Some drive-in theatres, once used for movies, are now being used for worship services. Worshipers can come in their pajamas if they like.

Today's secularism permeates and rises within each and every church. Within any congregation, members grow oblivious to what is taking place around them, becoming accustomed to and drawn by an ever-changing lifestyle. Standards are lowered, and the church in its quest for more members overlooks basic values and becomes like any other organization, just seeking bodies to enrich its rolls. As more and more yeast is added, the teachings of Jesus Christ become secondary. Churchgoing becomes another secular happening.

BORN-AGAIN BELIEVERS OR CHURCH ATTENDEES

Recently, I went to the funeral of a dear friend. The denomination of the church where she was eulogized and where her life was celebrated is irrelevant. Before attending the funeral, I read with interest the obituary, where it was written that she had been a member of a particular church for forty years. The year of her death was 2006, which meant that she had her name on this church's roll since 1966.

A son of the deceased was on the celebration program and he had this to say about his mother:

"I was saved in 1982, and it was then that I, being known for my previous mischievous ways, asked the Lord Jesus to save me. It was the next year that I went to visit with my Dad and Mom, only to find her on the couch crying. Dad, who was sitting in a chair close by, explained that Mom had been told today by her doctor that she would have to have heart-bypass surgery.

I went over to the couch, took Mom by the hand and asked, 'would you like to receive Jesus into your life?' She nodded in the affirmative as I got down on my knees to pray for her to receive Jesus.

Forgetting that Dad was in the room, I felt a touch of his hand on mine, and it was then that he also indicated that he wanted to receive Jesus also as his Savior. Both Mom and Dad received the Lord as their personal Savior that day.

Today, I know that I will see my Mom again in Heaven."

The calculator in my brain began to run the dates that he had mentioned. Didn't he say the year that his mother had been saved was 1983? That's only twenty-three years ago. But, the obituary had said that she had been a member of the church for forty years, which meant that she had been an unsaved churchgoer on a church's membership roll for seventeen years. Luckily, she had a son who knew the difference between salvation and churchgoing. Both of his parents had been long-time members of a church, but were not saved.

There are tens of millions of churchgoers and church members that fall into the same category, and each one has become the yeast that permeates the church.

Obituaries are written every day that begin by saying, "God called them home" or "they have gone to be with the Lord." We are living in a society where everyone wants, hopes, and wishes to go to Heaven. We want all our relatives, as well as ourselves, to end up there, but there will be only a few to find the narrow gate to His kingdom.

When a loved one is lying in a casket, our thoughts are that they can be no other place but heaven. We begin to weigh the good things that they did, while failing to see the bad things or the sins. The scales of good deeds against bad deeds will never balance and will come up weightless in the sight of God. Today's humanity has their thumb on the scale of good deeds trying to make the scale balance.

A person can stand on street corners in every city of the world, and can do good deeds of helping little old ladies across the street to safety. People can cook and serve meals to the needy, help the down-and-out, and give money to every beggar that asks. We can visit the prisons, hospitals, and assisted-living places. Not one good deed can wash away one of our sins. There is no way that goodness or mercy on our part can nullify or erase our sins. A philosophy of one good deed for one sin is not a workable solution to humanity's sin problem.

God turned Adam and Eve out of the Garden of Eden because of their sin of disobedience. No longer would God fellowship with them, because they were now sinful and had fallen. Because of their sinful nature, they were unable to enter into the presence of a Holy God. Adam and Eve were in perfect fellowship with God before their disobedience, but having become sinners, this fellowship had been broken.

The desire for the unsaved to attend church is an admirable one, but no one should be led into believing that a person is in the good graces of God by attending. Unsaved churchgoers are misleading themselves and others by professing and claiming Christianity. These infiltrators are only "leaning" toward Christianity while "leading" others away from the Christian movement. The unsaved on church rolls continue to be the yeast for their philosophies, beliefs, and cultural-oriented lifestyles.

Salvation from sins has yet to become a reality to these infiltrators of the Christian faith. Churchgoing and attendance, regular or irregular, become what the unsaved have been led to believe are the necessary cleansing tools for their sins.

The separation of saved believers from the unsaved will come when God separates "the sheep from the goats." Jesus said that weeds, which would be difficult to distinguish from the wheat, would grow within the crops and advised his followers to leave them alone, since God will do the separating. Christians are not to become like the "goats," but are to be separate and distinct. The Gospel, when preached today, falls on the ears of the saved as well as the unsaved. Hearts of the saved are opened—while the hearts of the unsaved remain dull and closed.

I once knew a farmer that took less care of his planted crops on unpaved back roads where there were few travelers, but on the main thoroughfare he paid very special attention to the maintenance of his crops. He wanted those who passed by on the more traveled roads to believe that he was a good farmer. As I travel the blue highways of America today, I see some fields with a tremendous number of weeds. The weeds overshadow the good crop just as the unsaved within the church overshadow the saved. The yeast of the unsaved continues to permeate.

CHRISTIANITY BRINGS LIFESTYLE CHANGES

When a non-churchgoing secular world sees friends, relatives, or coworkers joining a church, they expect some changes to take place in the lives of those now professing Christianity. As the new converts continue in their past lifestyles without making some noticeable changes, there is nothing to challenge the non-churchgoer, who is watching every move. The non-churchgoer sees only that the new "patches" of church attendance have been sewn on old garments.

Jesus was explicit in his teachings about a person having to be born again. He explained to Nicodemus the way to enter his kingdom. According to Jesus, it is necessary that a person be born again in order to enter His Kingdom. There is a human birth and a spiritual birth.

Jesus had many followers in his day and because of the harshness of his teachings, many deserted the ranks and went back to their old ways. They didn't continue to hang around, but went back to what they were doing after they were exposed to his teachings. Today's infiltrators are not being confronted with the teachings of Jesus, and continue to "hang around," while believing that this is what Christianity is about.

The unsaved who are sitting in the pews today are not being challenged by denominational leaders to account for their unbelief, and neither are they being challenged by local church bodies. Churches and religious bodies will forever strive to maintain the status quo of obtaining more members, because statistics can look good on paper.

Once inside a Christian church where the teachings of Jesus are being preached, members who are not saved can be saved. The answer to why the unsaved are not being saved today is threefold: The unsaved do not recognize their lost condition; the Gospel of Jesus Christ is not being preached; and God has called these unsaved so long that they have become stone-deaf to hearing and heart-dead to his wooing. The lost have heard the Gospel message many times, but have never responded.

The infiltration of the yeast of the unsaved into Christian churches is similar to that of a Christian young person who wants to be married to a person that professes no faith. The Bible teaches that Christians are not to be yoked together with unbelievers in marriage. A Christian might believe that upon entering a marriage to the unbeliever, through his or her influence, the one that is an unbeliever will accept their faith. No one has the strength or ability to change another, for only God, upon the willingness of a person, can make the changes. When Jesus is preached, God will do the work of saving the unsaved.

The irony about the unsaved within the ranks of churches today is that even though they were called, they were not chosen by Jesus, because of their insincerity. Non-believers "feel" the need for something spiritual, but the "feeling" isn't enough to bring commitment and saving faith. Drivers stop for traffic lights because it is a law. Unbelievers "stop in" at the church to relieve a "feeling" of need or for reasons of their own. The yeast of unbelieving infiltrators permeates and overshadows true believers and Christianity.

The unsaved come to fill the pews not for spiritual purposes but out of a need to be identified with Christianity and to get what they believe is their ticket to heaven. To them, the church brings the distinction of what Christianity represents and means to each home in a community. Churchgoing can easily become a community function, and still not be in the spiritual realm of worshiping God.

Grandparents and parents want their children basking in the religion they grew up with. Most feel the need to belong and be a part of something, and most want to believe that they are going to heaven when they die. We have become a nation of "group joiners." Just to be on the safe side, eggs are being put into several baskets in the hope that at death, all the bases have been covered. Infiltrators of the Christian faith need to travel the dusty roads with Jesus to come to an understanding of Christianity and its teachings.

MEDITATION

A TRIP BACK IN TIME

Being back home and having read from the Gospel according to Saint Luke, I asked my friend if he would again travel with me back in time to Jericho.

"Why Jericho?" he asked.

I responded by saying that it was the home of Zacchaeus, a short man who was a chief tax collector.

"Yes!" my friend responded, and off to Jericho we went.

Arriving in Jericho, we had no problem obtaining directions to the home of Zacchaeus. The city was vibrant and alive with excited people who were familiar with the chief tax collector. As we inquired about directions to his home, many offered unsolicited information about Zacchaeus.

"You should have been here yesterday and seen Zacchaeus up in that Sycamore tree," some were saying.

"We would never have thought that of him," someone remarked. "Here we were—fathers with children on our shoulders trying to get a glimpse of Jesus, and there was Zacchaeus, a very wealthy, influential, and despised man, up in that tree, exposing himself to ridicule."

"All of us wanted to see Jesus, but Zacchaeus was willing to go to greater extremes to rise above the crowds to see him," said one man. "And do you know what? It is said that when Jesus got to the tree that Zacchaeus had climbed, Jesus even called him by name, as if he knew him, and invited himself to go home with Zacchaeus."

"Yes!" said another man. "I was close to that tree and heard Jesus say: 'Zacchaeus! Come down from there immediately for I must stay with you today.'"

"Of course, we didn't approve of Jesus' choosing Zacchaeus to go eat with, because he is a tax collector and a sinner," said another. "We now hear that Zacchaeus has had a complete turnaround. We've been told that Zacchaeus, after meeting Jesus, is giving one-half of his possessions to the poor, and that he has promised to pay back four times any amount he cheated from us."

Continuing in the direction we had been pointed toward the home of Zacchaeus, we were approached by a woman who stopped to ask: "Are you looking for Zacchaeus?"

"Why, yes we are," we said.

"He is not at home," she said. "I'm his wife. He's out giving away our possessions."

"How do you feel about that?" I asked.

"It's great!" she said. "You see, I met Jesus, too. You don't meet Jesus without your life being changed."

— derived from Luke 19:1-10.

CHAPTER SIX

JESUS AND BAPTISM

"That if you will confess with your mouth, the Lord Jesus, and believe in your heart that God has raised him from the dead, you will be saved." Rom. 10:9

BAPTISM BY IMMERSION

Jesus, God in human form, walked on earth some two thousand years ago. He came on the scene just like every one of us, being born as a baby. His birth was different than ours: his mother was a virgin, and his father was the Holy Spirit. To some human ears that sounds like fantasy. But people of faith need only remember, "With God, all things are possible."

Jesus was fully human, and yet he was God. He came to teach us about God, for he was God, and to die on a cross for the sins of those who would believe in him. He fulfilled what he was sent to do, and did it without committing a sin. His presence enabled humankind to intimately know about his love and forgiveness for their wrongfulness.

Jesus was about thirty years old when he went to where John the Baptist was preaching and requested John's baptism. No one, except the religious doubters, could have been in the presence of Jesus without knowing that Jesus came from God. It is ironic that the religious parties were at odds with Him.

John the Baptist, recognizing his sinfulness in the presence of Godliness, told Jesus of his need of baptism. Jesus was in need of the baptism that John was offering, not because he was a sinner and in need of forgiveness, but because God meant for him to "fulfill all righteousness."

The baptizing done by John the Baptist was baptism of repentance and was done by immersion. After the ascension of Jesus, however, some religious bodies, denominations, and churches adopted sprinkling as a means of baptism. Baptism by sprinkling is not scriptural. Sprinkling cannot display to new converts in the faith or to witnesses the significance of the burying of an old life and being raised to walk in newness of a born-again life.

Jesus went down into the water and was buried within the streams of the river Jordan. John lifted him up, and the voice of God was heard to say, "This is my Son in whom I am well pleased." With baptism, Jesus signified his death on the cross; the burial and resurrection from death; and living eternally beyond the grave.

Christians preach their first sermon when they are baptized. Born-again believers go down into the water having been saved prior to being baptized. They testify to others that they are burying an old life and are being raised from the water to walk in newness of life. "Therefore if a man (person) be in Christ, he is a new creation. Old things will pass away, behold all things will become new." That is what the new life in Christ is about: becoming what God intended for us to be after the fall of humankind.

An Ethiopian eunuch was traveling from Jerusalem to his country when the Holy Spirit of God instructed Philip, who was in the midst of a revival, to go down into the desert to meet, teach, and counsel the eunuch. It was so important for God to have one sinner repent and be saved that he sent a busy, godly man to instruct another person about Jesus.

The eunuch, reading from the sayings of Isaiah, and not having the commentaries of today, was unable to understand what he was reading. Philip interpreted the passage for the eunuch, explaining that the prophet was talking about Jesus. The eunuch, seeing a body of water, asked of Philip, "What hinders me from being baptized?" The two of them went down into the water and the eunuch was baptized.

Baptism by sprinkling is just another diversion from the truths of the Bible. Some denominations attest to sprinkling, claiming that it was the New Testament way. The Ethiopian could have said to Philip, "See I have a container of water that I have brought along for drinking on my way across this desert, why not baptize me with it?"

The decision to sprinkle instead of to immerse is just one of many changes to Holy Scriptures over the ages. A religious leader is unable to bless water and make it holy water. Sprinkling was not the way that Jesus and converts were baptized in Biblical days.

BAPTISM FOLLOWS A PROFESSION OF FAITH

Baptism comes after repentance and confession of one's faith in the resurrected Christ. Some get the "cart before the horse" when it comes to baptism. Later in life, some may realize that when they were baptized, they were not saved. The question is often asked: "Should I now go back and get baptized again?" My answer to that question is, "Definitely!" Baptism might not be that important to some, but since salvation comes before being baptized, it should be important to every born-again person to do it the Biblical way.

There are many beliefs about baptism held by some denominations and churches. Some believe that the Holy

Spirit comes upon the believer at baptism, while some feel that a person is not saved until he or she has been baptized. Scriptures are oft-times quoted in attempts to prove such teachings. The important element is the salvation of the believer, and then baptism.

God does not need water to save those who have sincerely repented and trusted in the Cross for salvation. It is the blood of Jesus that washes away sins, not water. There have been battlefield confessions, deathbed confessions, and jailhouse confessions, where baptism by immersion never became a possibility for believers. Should they have had to await their salvation until water was available to them? Certainly not!

A study of the Scriptures tells us that God doesn't need water in addition to the blood that was poured out at Calvary. Baptism for believers is what is done in obedience to what Jesus has done for every person who believes in him. "Therefore go and make disciples of all nations, baptizing them in the name of the Father, and of the Son, and of the Holy Spirit."

John the Baptist and Jesus came into the world with two different purposes: John was sent to prepare the way for the Messiah, and Jesus' purpose was to be the perfect and complete sacrifice for the sins of humanity. John's message was one of repentance, for the kingdom of Heaven is at hand. Jesus' message was, "For the Son of Man came to seek and to save what was lost."

Hearts appear to be as hardened today as they were in the days of the Pharisees and Sadducees. Beliefs don't fit into the mold of the One who would proclaim, "I am the way, the truth, and the life.... no one comes to God except through me." People come today with skepticism and unbelief, questioning everything that is not before them in black and white. It is not with the mind that Jesus is found, but with faith and contrite hearts. Realizing the need of a cleansing from sins, sinners come with repentance in their hearts believing that Jesus can do for them what they can never do for themselves.

Baptism has nothing to do with salvation, but is solely in obedience to the Lord and the following of Him in baptism. It is a visible act by born-again believers in letting others know to whom they belong. Baptism without salvation means only that we go into the water as a sinner and come out a wet sinner. Only the blood of Jesus, and not water, washes away sins.

Jesus, after his baptism, immediately went into a forty-day period of fasting. He was tempted and tested by the devil, often quoting Scripture to fend off the wiles of his tempter. The devil made many overtures and promises, and when it was over, angels came and ministered to Jesus' needs. Because Jesus was human, temptations throughout his life came at other times for Jesus, just as they come today to those who are his followers.

The devil never gives up on born-again believers, for he is trying to pull them away from God. He comes in many forms, fashions, disguises, and voices, trying to get a fallen people to worship him and to stray from God. He appears in the home, the pews, the workplace, in a smile, a flirtation, and in the friendly or suggestive gestures of another person.

JESUS AND HIS TEACHINGS

Immediately after the temptation, Jesus began to choose his disciples. His disciples did not choose him. God is the one that does the choosing, just as he is the one that does the choosing with those today that are called to be Christians or disciples. "Many are called but few are chosen." It is a dreadful situation to feel His calling and to turn away. Some say: "I'll wait until I get better or get something behind me, or wait until next time!"

It's impossible to come at one's convenience, for that time may never come again. Jesus told his disciples "no one can come to the Father, unless God draws them." Sinners will know when they are being drawn, and some with knuckles tight, hold onto the pews and never let go.

Jesus carried on a thirty-six-months-plus ministry with his disciples, teaching them the things that they would be doing in his name after the crucifixion. He taught them in straight forward language and often in parables. On several occasions he was asked to explain his teachings, especially about some of his parables.

Jesus' teachings were God-sent, and his disciples and other listeners could not spiritually comprehend the words that came out of the mouth of the Son of God. Jesus knew that the complete understanding by his hearers of his teachings would not come at the moment, but would follow after his death on the Cross when God's Holy Spirit would provide the insight.

Today, we read from the pages of the written Word, and don't always fully understand what some verses mean. An innumerable number of concordances, books, and dictionaries attempt to decipher the words of Jesus. God provides to each believer, upon their conversion experience, the Holy Spirit to give the necessary assistance to discern the Scriptures. Through prayer and the Bible, a person can get closer to the One "who gave his life as a ransom for many."

The message that Jesus brought to the world is not a complicated one, for it is a message composed of faith. It takes only the simple faith of a child to come to an understanding of what it is to believe in Him. Doctorates and undergraduate degrees are not necessary. The true way to find out what is truth and fiction in Christianity is to read the pages of the Bible under the leadership of God's Holy Spirit. God speaks to individuals from out of his Word.

MEDITATION

A TRIP BACK IN TIME

My friend and I were impressed with what we had seen and heard in these back-in-time trips and were determined to visit often. In Galilee, we soon caught up with two of John the Baptist's disciples, who had been instructed by John to deliver a message to Jesus. We closed ranks with them to hear John's message to Jesus.

"Are you the one who was to come, or should we expect someone else?" John wanted an answer to some doubts that he was now having. Prison had turned into a lonely place, and John, even more isolated and apart from "being the voice of one crying out in the wilderness," wanted an answer to his question. Doubts will always be put into our hearts and minds by the devil. And the devil was working on John.

As the question was asked of Jesus, my friend and I, along with the others, waited patiently for an answer from Jesus. Would he enter into a detailed explanation, trying to prove to them that he was the Christ or would he defer to Andrew or perhaps John, two of John's disciples that had left John the Baptist's ranks to follow Jesus?

Would Jesus say, "How about it, Andrew, do you think that I am the Messiah? Do you want to leave and go back to John? Do you think that someone else will be coming along that you will prefer over me? Tell your former companions who you think that I am." Or would he place the two inquirers on hold, saying that he was too busy to be interrupted?

We had caught Jesus at a very busy time, for still lingering near him were the blind that could now see, those who had never heard but could now hear, and those who had never walked, staring in disbelief at John's disciples. Those that had been healed appeared to open their mouths, supposedly wanting to answer the question that had been asked of Jesus. It was then that Jesus' gaze shifted to the recipients of his grace as he answered:

"Go back and report to John what you hear and see," said Jesus.

Jesus had spoken, and there was no further need for us to linger. As we were leaving, we could hear in the background the voice of Jesus as he began to talk about John the Baptist:

"This is the one about whom it is written: I will send my messenger ahead of you, who will prepare your way before you. I tell you the truth. Among those born of women there has not risen anyone greater than John the Baptist . . ."

It would be on our next trip that my friend and I would hear that John the Baptist's head had been delivered on a platter to the daughter of Herodias.

—derived from Matthew 11:1-15.

CHAPTER SEVEN

INFILTRATION: EARLY BIBLICAL TIMES

"In those days Peter stood up among the believers (a group numbering about a hundred and twenty)" Acts 1:15

BELIEVERS IN JERUSALEM AWAIT THE PROMISE

A few days before the ascension of Jesus, Peter went fishing with six of Jesus' disciples. Having nothing to show for their fishing expedition, the disciples brought their boat near to the shore where their risen Lord awaited them.

Jesus called out to them: "Friends, haven't you any fish?"

"No," they answered.

"Throw your net on the right side of the boat and you will find some," said Jesus.

A few days after this, Peter stood up to address the first recorded assembly of Christians, a group of one hundred twenty believers. Unbelievers had yet to infiltrate this group which was being obedient to the commands of Jesus to wait.

67

Jesus had ministered to most of them for three years or more, and they were now waiting as they had been told to do. While they waited, they appointed a replacement for Judas Iscariot, the apostle that had betrayed Jesus.

These one hundred twenty persons, now with heavy hearts, had personally had an encounter with the Lord Jesus. No one had to tell them about Jesus—they had seen him with their eyes, and had heard his teachings about what the costs would be for them to be followers. The humanity of Jesus was gone, but their personal involvement with Jesus would forever remain in their memories. Each one would have an experience or a memory to share with others about their relationship with the Lord.

This meeting of the group of believers had not been turned into a wake, since Jesus was not in some graveyard, but was alive, having risen from the dead only a few days before. In keeping with the instructions of Jesus, they were staying together and getting prepared for whatever lay before them. They were doing what Jesus wants every believer to do, to be ready when he calls.

Having been instructed to wait in Jerusalem "for the gift that my Father has promised," these believers were waiting for the promise to be fulfilled. The Holy Spirit that was coming was to be not only for them, but for all future believers.

The wait would not be for long, for suddenly the sound of a raging wind filled the house and what seemed to be tongues of fire separated and came to rest on each of them. All of them were filled with the Holy Spirit and began to speak in other tongues as the Spirit enabled them.

God-fearing Jews who were visiting Jerusalem from every known nation heard the Gospel being preached in their language by the one hundred twenty believers. God had provided the setting, the audience, the message, and the power. Before the day ended, about three thousand believers were added to their number. The gate to repentance, faith, and salvation in the name of Jesus was now open, and like mighty wind-tossed oceans, these believers, and those that would follow, would touch every inhabited shoreline with His message.

After receiving the Holy Spirit, the small group of believers continued to preach about Jesus in the streets of Jerusalem and the surrounding localities. Having been told by Jesus to evangelize the world, and having seen the power of God in the raising of Jesus, and being recipients of the Holy Spirit, they went about carrying out His commands. The ensuing persecutions enabled them to take their message throughout the known world.

As these followers went out to witness, miracles were performed through the power that had been given to them from above. These believers, because of their faith in the Risen One, "turned the world upside down." As Jesus was preached, not only believers, but some unbelievers who wanted to be like the believers, entered the ranks of Christianity.

THE UNSAVED AMONG THE SAVED

Believers were experiencing repentance, faith, and salvation, while unbelievers were captivated by the power of God in the lives of the believers. Some began to join the movement out of curiosity, desiring to participate in a movement where power and passion were being demonstrated.

Infiltrators were being attracted to the Christian movement for several reasons. Some saw the joy of the believers and the compassion that they had for others. Others, being motivated by leaders within the movement and their persuasiveness, came into the movement to follow the leader and not the Christ.

Some wanted the power that these early Christians were displaying in driving out demons and healing the sick. Unbelievers were motivated to join the movement for their own personal reasons, but not out of repentance and faith in a Risen Lord. These miraculous acts were enticements for the unsaved to permeate the ranks of the saved. There will always be "joiners" in any movement where something awesome is happening.

Apollos, a Jew from Alexandria, a learned man and great orator, came to Ephesus preaching and teaching about Jesus. He had many followers, and had a thorough knowledge of the Scriptures, as do many who preach the gospel today, but he had not been saved. He knew only the baptism of John the Baptist until Priscilla and Aquila, who were true believers, "explained the way of God more adequately." Apollos didn't have the big picture of Jesus, yet was preaching Jesus. Priscilla and Aquila took Apollos aside and explained to him how to be saved. Churches today are in need of born-again believers who can "explain the way of God more adequately to those who have infiltrated their ranks."

During these times, some people who claimed to be Christians went about invoking the name of Jesus in their efforts to drive out evil spirits. It is recorded in Acts that as the name of Jesus was being used by some unbelievers, the evil spirit answered them, "Jesus I know, and I know about Paul, but who are you?"

The world today is asking those who are claiming the name of Jesus, "Do you know the One whose name you are using?" The name of Jesus Christ is often used in the secular world in a profane way by those who profess him as well as those who don't. There is no reverence for Him or His name when it is being used in place of a four-letter word.

CHOOSING TO FOLLOW OTHERS INSTEAD OF JESUS

"Do your best to come to me quickly," wrote Paul to Timothy, "for Demas, because he loved this world, has deserted me and has gone to Thessalonica." Demas, Paul's traveling companion, had left the faith, going back to his old ways. Some will enter for awhile and leave, while others remain, wearing a Christian garment only on Sunday.

Paul, the apostle, wrote letters to churches about those who were now infiltrating their ranks with their own doctrines and who were not true converts to the faith. Churchgoers who had been converted were being swept up into the philosophies of the unbeliever. Churches had been evangelized, but had not been taught the precepts of Jesus' teachings. To be called Christian, churches have to follow the precepts of Jesus, because he is the founder.

It is evident from the writers of the New Testament that unbelievers were bringing their lifestyles and beliefs into the Christian assemblies. Some infiltrators came into the churches only to disrupt, confuse, and bring dissension among the believers.

Some members of these first- century churches wanted to be identified with their Christian leaders. Some claimed allegiance to Paul or to Apollos or to Cephas. Claims were being made by some that they were baptized by these leaders, and they belonged to them. Their obedience was to these leaders, just as some people in today's churches are preacher and denominational led instead of being saved by the preaching of the Word.

It is evident that unbelievers were among believers in the letters written in the Book of Revelation to the seven churches in the province of Asia. The Lord Jesus had a warning for these churches to get in true fellowship with Him.

The pages of the Bible mention only a few Pharisees who became interested in knowing about whether Jesus was the Messiah. The so-called religious of that time period were thoroughly entrenched in their religious traditions and had become unshakeable. The Sadducees denied resurrection after death and, therefore, opposed the Christian movement with their dogmatic beliefs.

The infiltration of unbelievers into Christianity since the first century increases every year as the population of the world increases. From the teachings of the Apostles to the Reformation and beyond, religious bodies and denominations have incorporated their own precepts and teachings into the Christian movement. New religious bodies spring up; new denominations are formed; churches split; churches die; new ones are formed; new teachings occur; new interpretations emerge, and all in the name of Christianity. A watering-down of the Gospel of Jesus Christ by these religious venues attracts inquisitors to their doors. The results: more people are being misled, and more infiltrators are led into believing that they are following Christianity and its teachings.

During the exodus from Egypt, the Israelites wandered around in the wilderness for forty years because of their disobedience and unbelief. There were only two from that generation that were permitted to enter the promised land. Because of this large number that was denied entry into the promised land, should there be any doubt that only three out of ten claiming Christianity today will enter Heaven?

After typing on my computer and getting ready to exit Microsoft Office Word, these questions always appear: "Do you want to keep the changes made to this document?" Yes? No? Having made many changes, and spending a considerable amount of time making those changes, I certainly don't want to lose it. If for some reason, I inadvertently hit the "No" instead of the "Yes," I will have lost what I intended to save. That is what will happen to unbelievers within the church. They will lose the heaven that they thought they had by their churchgoing and attempts at Christianity. All of "their efforts" will be in vain without repentance, faith, and the acceptance of the Lord Jesus.

MEDITATION

A TRIP BACK IN TIME

As we traveled back in time, our clothing changed to the attire of those that we would be walking among. The Holy Spirit would be interceding for us, not only interpreting our language to those we met, but interpreting what would be spoken to us. What we would speak in English would be received in Aramaic, Hebrew, or Greek. What we would hear from those that spoke to us or what we would overhear, would be heard in English. Our journey entirely depended on the presence of the Holy Spirit. That is very true of a person's life as a Christian.

My friend and I arrived in Jerusalem the afternoon that Jesus was crucified. Back home in the United States, we had come to know this day as "Good Friday." We immediately went out to a place called Golgotha, which means the Place of the Skull, since we were hearing that Jesus and two thieves were being crucified this very day.

Standing a good distance from the three crosses, we looked into the faces of the men and women that had gathered, trying to read by their expressions those who might have been friends or followers of Jesus. There were some women near to where we were standing, and as we moved closer to some of them, we were able to overhear bits and pieces of their chatter.

One of the women turned to another and said, "The hearts of my sons, John and James, are breaking today for they truly loved Jesus. My heart is aching not only for my sons, but for Jesus."

"Do you suppose that woman is the wife of Zebedee and the mother of James and John?" my friend asked.

"She must be," I said.

Turning our eyes toward the three crosses laid out on the ground, we saw Jesus and the two criminals, one on his left and the other on his right, being nailed to the crosses. It was then, glancing back to Mary, that I saw the agony on her face and tried to imagine what must be going through her mind. Not only must she be grieving for Jesus and his suffering, but for her sons, James and John, who could easily have been there on each side of Jesus.

Surely, this is not what she had wanted for her sons when she had asked Jesus to let her sons sit on his right and left when he came into His Kingdom. Was this the cup that Jesus had spoken of, and what about the kingdom he had talked about? Her thoughts surely went back to that day when she had gone to Jesus, and kneeling down before him, asked a favor.

"What is it you want?" he had asked.

"Grant that one of these two sons of mine may sit at your right and the other at your left in your kingdom," she had replied.

"You don't know what you are asking," Jesus said to them. "Can you drink the cup I am going to drink?"

"We can," they had answered.

Mary, standing in view of the cross, must now have nothing but gratitude in her heart that Jesus had dismissed her request. "Was this the cup?" she must be pondering. She certainly didn't have a cross in mind when she had gone to Jesus with her request. Jesus was certainly right when he had said that they didn't know what they were asking.

It was then that we heard a whisper of a prayer coming from the heart and lips of Mary: "Thank you God, that you don't give us everything that we ask for, and help us to realize that we aren't to follow you for what we can get out of it."

(James was later put to death for his faith, and John was exiled). It is costly to follow Jesus.

—derived from Matthew 20:20-28; 27:55-56.

CHAPTER EIGHT

THE DILUTION OF CHRISTIANITY (Part 1)

"People will be lovers of themselves, lovers of money, boastful, proud, abusive, disobedient to their parents, ungrateful, unholy,". . ."having a form of godliness, but denying its power . . ." 2 Tim. 3:2,5a.

CHRISTIANITY'S UNBIBLICAL ALTERATIONS

From the first century to the twenty-first century the message of God as recorded in the Scriptures has not been altered by God. There will not be any alterations, because the God of yesterday is the God of today. Humanity has made its own alterations to the precepts and teachings of God to adhere to their lifestyles. Religious bodies, in order to appease the masses of unbelievers within the pews of their sanctuaries, have done their own dilution of the Word of God.

A thorough watering-down of the message of the Bible has taken place over the past two thousand years, bringing untold numbers of unsaved persons into Christian bodies.

Since the earthly life of Jesus, many concepts and beliefs have been developed and put into practice by the masses. The message of repentance, faith, and conversion has been sacrificed for social programs, and a do-unto-others type religion.

Jesus' sacrifice for our sins made it possible for every believer to come into the presence of God. On the day of his crucifixion, "the curtain of the temple was torn in two from top to bottom" allowing every person an audience with God. No longer would it be necessary for any person to have to go through an earthly person or institution to be blessed, forgiven, or to have fellowship and prayer with God. The doorway to God was now open for anyone to come into His presence.

Since the crucifixion of Jesus, religious groups, denominations, and kings have proclaimed their authority by making changes to the Word of God in supporting their beliefs and lifestyles. Though manmade alterations and teachings have occurred, the Holy Bible, as written and inspired by God, remains the same. The Holy Scriptures will not support the many "offshoot" philosophies that some denominational groups are teaching and practicing as Christianity. Religious groups and cults have come and some have gone, but the Word of God remains vibrant and powerful to save.

After the Protestant Reformation, many denominations and religious bodies came forth with their interpretations about the teachings of the Bible. Within these religious groups there were some cults. There are many versions of the Bible, and some are closer to the Hebrew and Greek writings than others, because of the manuscripts that were used.

Not trying to be facetious, today's Christianity reminds me of why there are so many flavors in JELL-O. No doubt, it's because people have different tastes for secular lifestyles contrary to the one that was presented by Jesus to his followers. Manufacturers of consumer products have taken on the same type of merchandising for their products. One can purchase many kinds of tastes and colors within the same product. So it is with churches: If one doesn't like the teachings of one denomination, there are many opportunities to try another denomination and its teachings. Some denominations believe that for the ordinance of baptism, one can be sprinkled, while others hold to the belief of immersion. Some churches believe in missions, while others do not. Some have a taste for musical instruments, while others believe that you can sing praises without the help of manmade instruments. Some believe in foot washing, while others find it degrading. Undoubtedly, one could go on and on with these many facets within Christianity, since these are not the only differences that separate denominations from each other. A Christianity of convenience has come forth from these many denominational groupings and religious bodies.

This religion of convenience that is being called Christianity, and being practiced and preached in many denominations as being scriptural, is not about "love the Lord, your God with all your heart and with all your soul and with all your mind." The sins of today are not any different from the sins that God hated and punished from the beginning of time. It is true that God is a forgiving God and will forgive any sin other than that of the rejection of His Son, but those who willingly sin and continue to live in sin without remorse are living in danger of the fires of hell.

The Bible teaches that we should not condone the sins of those claiming Christianity who are "sexually immoral or greedy, an idolater or a slanderer, a drunkard or a swindler."

The immoral list grows longer as Paul warns about "sexual immorality, impurity and debauchery; idolatry and witchcraft, hatred, discord, jealousy, fits of rage, ambition, dissensions, factions and envy; drunkenness, orgies, and the like. I warn you, as I did before, that those who live like this will not inherit the kingdom of God."

Jesus died to wash away our sins and to make us acceptable to God. The depth of God's hatred for sin is evidenced in the destruction of Sodom and Gomorrah, where five righteous people could not be found. When men sent from God came to warn Lot and his family to flee the city, the men of the city tried to have sex with them. Marriage between homosexuals and lesbians is being sought legally through the courts today. And homosexuals are being placed in ministerial rolls in some denominations and churches.

MILLIONS PREFER TO REWRITE SOME BIBLICAL PASSAGES

Those within the gay movement, as well as others, believe that the Bible is out-of-date and doesn't cover the modernization of the times. They fail to understand that homosexuals have been a part of culture since the time of Abraham. Homosexuality was prevalent when the apostle Paul wrote his letter to the Romans. What has been forgotten is "that God is the same yesterday, today, and forever," and hasn't changed with today's lifestyles, feelings, and the beliefs of the masses.

God didn't put two males or two females in the Garden of Eden. Marriage was intended from the very beginning of time to be between a male and a female, and they were to become one flesh, forsaking all others. Men and women live together today without marriage and commitments, deciding to go separate ways when it doesn't work out. Pre-martial sex was not the intention of God. Today's culture tries to write its own laws, believing that "everyone is doing it" is justification for their actions.

Children are still being abused and have been sexually abused by priests and ministers throughout the ages. The media regularly reports scandals about supposedly godly men who have been removed from their pulpits because of ungodly sexual abuse of their bodies with those of the same sex. Recently, a well-known minister, Ted Haggard, was removed from his senior minister role at a mega-church with fourteen thousand members because of trysts with a person of the same sex. He voiced his opinion against homosexuality in the pulpit, but outside the confines of the church, his actions were not the same as his words.

Some churches don't condone the behavior of gay people and speak out against it. Some have begun to disallow membership to those who openly profess homosexuality. Churches in doing this are not in hatred of these individuals, but in hatred of their immoral acts. These churches are not being indifferent to gay people any more than they would ask a drunkard, abuser, wife beater, thief, or anyone to depart from their immoral ways. True believers are to come into a new life, leaving old ways behind them.

Should there be a way for born-again believers to reflect a light that would shine in the total darkness of an overflowing sanctuary, it would be difficult today for those entering to find enough light to guide them to a pew. The darkness of unbelievers sitting in the pews of the majority of churches today in America would overshadow the light. Christianity has been diluted and watered-down so much during these two thousand years, that it is becoming more and more difficult to recognize true believers.

CHAPTER NINE

THE DILUTION OF
CHRISTIANITY (Part 2)

CHURCHGOING INSTEAD OF
CHRISTIANITY BEING PRACTICED

Christianity has been the predominant religion in the
United States since the establishment of this nation.
The claim has been made throughout this land that we are a
Christian nation. Church doors swing open every weekend
for believers and unbelievers to enter. Only fire marshals
care whether the doors swing in or out, but to the tens of
millions that are entering these doors, it is important that
churchgoers, claiming the name of Jesus, act and live the
lives of born-again believers.

Ancestors have led the masses into believing that
"churchgoing" is the most important element in being in the
good graces of God, and is the primary way to reach heavenly portals. Today's children will engage in the practices
of their forefathers, and will teach the same philosophy to
their children and future generations. By attending church,
we appear to others to be Christians, but it has only become
a routinely traditional way of life.

What is being taught in the home today is not so much about Jesus, but is about the churches in the community. The circle of churchgoing beliefs will never be broken until parents tell their children about the salvation offered by Jesus. Parents are guilty of having put their mark on their descendants by leading them to believe that churchgoing is a prerequisite to heaven. Children that grow up in the church soon come to believe that repentance, faith, and salvation are not the ingredients they need. By living in the church all of their lives, they question what they have done wrong, and ask, "Why is there a need for confession?"

Recently I read where a mother's fifteen-year-old daughter had become pregnant. The mother was upset with the public school system because it had not taught sex education classes to her daughter. The mother had neglected to discuss sex with her daughter, feeling that it was the school system's responsibility. Parents not only neglect this responsibility about sex education, but are failing their children when it comes to educating them about the teachings of the Bible.

Glancing out the window, I see three trees that I recently planted. Those trees will become one of the marks that I will leave for my descendants for as long as they live. My remaining loved ones will share with their children and grandchildren information about who planted those trees. The shadow of those limbs will fall upon those who will come to admire them. The marks of a parent's beliefs will rest and abide with their children as they pass on their beliefs to them. If Jesus is taught as the primary reason for going to church, Jesus and the Cross will bring repentance to those seeking God. If churchgoing is taught, then churchgoing will be where the emphasis is placed. Children will think that what was good for Mama and Papa is good enough for them.

Parents who are knowledgeable of the Scriptures and its teaching will lead their children into the knowledge of the Lord Jesus. Parents who are trying to keep the tradition of churchgoing, and are only teaching their children to remember the Lord's Day and to keep it holy, are worshiping the law and not the Giver of the law. When only the concept of churchgoing is taught and practiced, parents will inevitably mislead their children into becoming infiltrators of the faith.

The dilution of Christianity has occurred throughout the ages. Every generation departs further and further from God and His teachings. In my lifetime, secularism has drawn the masses into believing that all things can be good, and that there is no harm in participating. The philosophy is that "if it makes you happy, then why not indulge as long as it makes you feel good."

THE REMOVAL OF CHRISTIANITY FROM THE WORKPLACE

The removal of God from our culture causes our moral behavior and ethical attitudes to become dim and blurred. Although we might consider our nation Christian, born-again believers are completely failing to put into practice Christian behavior. True believers are beginning to be misled by the actions of unbelievers within churches, and the "yeast" will continue to grow.

Employers could at one time ask on their applications about an applicant's religious beliefs. Their thinking was that if you were a Christian or affiliated with a church, you were going to work harder and be honest, and that your morals were going to be above reproach. This caused some to affiliate with churches, whether saved or not, because jobs at that time were not plentiful.

When I was a child, some teachers on Mondays asked if I had gone to church the previous Sunday. It was embarrassing to go to school and not be able to respond in the affirmative. Therefore, I went to church occasionally so that I could raise my hand on Monday morning. It was many years later that I became a born-again believer. Some parents, especially those who don't want their children exposed to any concept pertaining to God, don't want the mention of God to be made in any setting.

In today's culture, the days are gone when a teacher or an employer could ask anything about an applicant's religious beliefs. Because of the threat of being sued or being offensive to those of different or no beliefs, the name of God has been taken out of the schools and the workplace.

Christianity was deeply rooted in bygone days when people depended more on God rather than on material things. Secular activities, sexual appetites, and ungodly pursuits have replaced some of our dependence on a Supreme Being. One person, by going to the courts, is capable of telling the majority in America that they can't bring their religious beliefs into the world of secularism. The vocal minority outshouts the silent majority.

Christians aren't to be offensive and intolerant to those of other faiths or to those who don't believe in God. The lifestyles of born-again believers have to be their testimony. Anything that refers to a Supreme Being has been or will eventually be removed from public places due to the apathy of born-again believers. The day is fast approaching when even a private property owner will have to have a permit to display anything on his property that alludes to God.

Regardless of these constraints, Christianity remains the number one choice of religions among Americans. But it has become more of a tradition handed down by our ancestors than an abiding faith in Jesus Christ.

Traveling the interstates and the blue highways of America, we see steeples with their crosses reaching into the heavens. Crucifixes are worn around necks and ankles, and are tattooed on biceps and elsewhere on the body. Billboards dot the countryside with the message of Christianity. Some inmates within the walls of detention centers and prisons weave and wear crosses around their necks to display their belief. Whether fashionable or religious, Americans still want to display to the world their faith in Christianity. Wearing or displaying a cross or worshiping under a cross, however, doesn't make a person a Christian. Persons who commit horrendous crimes wear crosses and confess the name of Christ. Some are born-again believers while others remain in the ranks of the unsaved or infiltrators.

THE QUEST FOR NUMBERS

Denominations go against denominations and churches go against churches competing for members. And when inviting someone to church, the invitation is "come and hear our preacher" or "we have a program to meet every need." Have you ever heard or have you ever been invited to visit a church by having someone say to you, "Come and feel the presence of Jesus or come and worship God and give Him praise?"

A church is the easiest and least costly place in the United States where a person can become a member. Churches don't have initiation fees or monthly dues. Very few will be told that the church will be expecting a lot from them, and in some cases will be handed a few pamphlets explaining church membership. When a person says that he or she is a Christian or has someone put words into his or her mouth, membership in most churches becomes obtainable.

Many churches are so eager to add names to their rolls that the prerequisite of salvation for membership is forgotten.

There are no dues, "just offerings and tithes or whatever the Lord lays on your heart to give." The minister appears to be doing his or her job when people are walking the aisle and joining the church. Enlargement of the church rolls will enhance a minister's resume and increase the chances of his or her moving on to a more attractive and rewarding parsonage.

The dilution of Christianity has come a long way since the day of Pentecost. The early Christians met, shared, sacrificed, rejoiced, were of one accord, and proclaimed the name of a Savior that had been crucified, buried, raised, yet still lives, and was coming again. Ask someone today who is the "Head of the Church," and that person might name the Pope, the preacher, or some influential deacon down at the local congregation. Were the early churches perfect churches? No, there were unbelievers even then, but they were in the minority. Saved believers who will forever remain imperfect should now be striving for perfection.

There is a lot of confusion among society today about how one can become a Christian, and about what a Christian really is. Ask individuals out on the streets of America to define the word "Christian" and be prepared for the many definitions that will flow from the lips of those who say that they are Christians. Many and varied are the answers that will be given to the question of "how does one become a Christian?" Most of those being asked such a question will not have gone inside a sanctuary for weeks.

Christianity is not about having our names on church rolls or attending worship services, nor is it about meeting people that can do a person the most good in the secular world. Christianity is about conviction, repentance, faith, salvation, and the turning away from sin and a turning to God.

Churchgoing without salvation through the Cross of Jesus means very little to the unbeliever. Churchgoing may help people feel better about themselves and others, but it is about each individual having a personal relationship with God through the Lord Jesus Christ.

Many people have been turned off by the actions of individuals in churches who are calling themselves Christians, but whose actions and deeds are far from a reflection of a Savior who said "follow me." We have heard it said: "if that is what Christianity is all about, then I want no part of it."

Churchgoers should read and study the New Testament and discover and define their thinking of what and who a Christian is, to see if it coincides with their beliefs. This would provide the opportunity for readers to rethink their faith and to evaluate their relationship with the Lord. The apostle Paul called Christians to evaluate themselves.

The devil has done a very deceitful job in helping unbelievers to believe that they are Christians by means other than the Cross.

Church leaders and leaders of religious bodies are condoning the infiltration of unbelievers into their ranks. They are playing the numbers game by not wanting to give up the contributions that come from the ranks of unbelievers. Tithes, offerings, and contributions don't make an unbeliever a believer. About ten percent of those who are members of a congregation give seventy-five percent of the money collected. The other ninety percent give twenty-five percent of the rest. "Where your treasure is—there will be your heart."

Nothing will ever be done by religious bodies to rid their rolls of unbelievers, and to stop this dilution, unless Jesus is preached. Only Jesus is "able to save to the uttermost those that believe." It is he who will "separate the sheep from the goats," as "the tares continue among the wheat."

Those who are lost know their true spiritual condition if they have read and studied the Bible, and have been under the preaching of the Cross. Will they purge themselves from

Christianity or remain seated in padded pews? It will be difficult to change the attitudes and embedded beliefs that have
shaped the thinking and upbringing of generations. It will
happen only when hearts under conviction and repentance
allow God to make the necessary changes.

Am I one of the diluters of the Christian faith? Am
I diluting the teachings of Jesus by the way that I act and
behave before others? Those are questions that all persons
claiming the name of Jesus should ask of themselves.

MEDITATION

A TRIP BACK IN TIME

Back in time, my friend and I went to talk with the wealthy
young man who had asked Jesus: "Teacher, what good thing
must I do to get eternal life?" We caught up with the young
man early in the afternoon in Judea near the Jordan River.
Just a few hours before, in the early morning hours, this rich
young man had spent some time with Jesus.

The young man was not pleased with our invasion of his
space and asked if we could come back another day. "Oh!"
he said, "I will be happy to talk with you another time, but
for now, I'm not in the mood for talking or sharing my time
with others."

"We were just passing through here, and this will be
the only time that we have before leaving," we explained.
"Please give us a few minutes of your time."

"Oh, okay!" he said. "Just what is it that you want to talk
with me about? Also, please remember that you have said 'a
few minutes.'"

"We understand that you and Jesus talked with each other
this morning, and wanted to know about what was said. How
did things go?" we asked.

"Jesus invited me to join his group of disciples and to follow him," he said.

"Why, then, are you so sad and why so depressed? We would think that it would be an honor and a privilege to follow someone who is doing so much good," we commented.

"The price was too high," he said.

"Do you mean that Jesus was asking money from you in order to follow him?" we asked.

"No! No! Not for him, but for the poor. He wanted me to give all of my possessions away, before following him. That would be an awful price for me to pay. I have been a good man all of my life, and what I wanted to do was to do some more good to have this eternal life that Jesus is talking about. I've worked hard for my money and to get to where I am and it's very important to me," he said.

"Then why are you so sad?" we wanted to know.

"I don't know if I've made the right decision," he said. "Anyway, regardless of my choice, I will keep adding to my wealth while seeking to find another way to enter eternal life. Perhaps someone else will come along to offer me a more reasonable solution to my dilemma. I can't afford to leave the life that I am enjoying, and to start over again."

Bidding goodbye to the young man, we, too, departed in sadness from his presence. We had read where Jesus had told his disciples: "It is easier for a camel to go through the eye of a needle than for a rich man to enter the kingdom of God."

Arriving back in the twenty-first century, we were in agreement that not only riches but other things often come between people and God. We could not shake from our minds the saddest words spoken by the rich young man: "Perhaps someone else will come along to offer me a more reasonable solution to my dilemma."

It was then that we remembered the question that Jesus asked of the twelve on another occasion: "You do not want to leave too, do you?" Simon Peter responded for the rest of the group by saying, "Lord, to whom shall we go? You have the words of eternal life. We believe and know that you are the Holy One of God."

—derived from Matthew 19:16-24.

CHAPTER TEN

JUDAS: THE FIRST INFILTRATOR

". . . Teacher, I will follow you wherever you go."
Matt. 19:20b

JUDAS: AN UNBELIEVER

The infiltration of the unsaved into the Christian faith began with Judas Iscariot. He was one of the twelve chosen by Jesus, becoming one of the twelve apostles. There were others that followed Jesus for awhile, but left before the crucifixion because of the harsh teachings that they were hearing. Jesus' words of "count the cost," as well as other stipulations, caused many to turn back.

Jesus walked on many dusty roads in the brief time that he was here. He went to where the people were. He asked for total commitment from those that would follow him, just as he is asking total commitment today. His teachings have not changed, but have been modified to suit those within a culturally oriented society.

How would it be at your local church if Jesus were the pastor? And what would be the reaction of the membership?

I see Jesus standing before a pulpit committee and being denied a trial sermon or being told by a bishop, deacon, or elder that the church where he is serving no longer wants him as their pastor. I see those that have infiltrated Christianity leaving the pews and returning to their secular world, should Jesus become and remain their pastor.

The cool water from the Jordan and the Sea of Galilee washed away the dust from the body of the Master and came in waves of refreshment to a tired and sometimes lonely man where crowds consistently followed him. It was on one of those dusty roads that Jesus met up with Judas Iscariot and chose him as one of his disciples.

Judas must have been elated when he was appointed the treasurer of the group, because he could see the potential opportunity. With large crowds following Jesus, there would be times when money would flow into the treasury. Just like today, when initial public offerings make their appeal to investors on the New York Stock Exchange, Judas' selection to become a follower of Jesus, appeared to Judas as an initial investment of his time to a promising opportunity. There is no way to know what was in the heart of Judas or to know his intentions. Whatever the reasons, Judas accepted Jesus' invitation to join the group.

Judas became the forerunner for the masses who have over the centuries infiltrated Christianity. Judas had his reasons for being a part of Christianity and so do others who are unsaved and within the church. "Many are called, but few are chosen."

JESUS: A MESSAGE OF DISCIPLESHIP

There was not, during the humanity of Jesus, the rush of the masses to become true followers. Many came to hear his message, partake of the miracles, eat the provided food, and to hear his words. Only eleven of his followers were there when he walked into the Garden of Gethsemane, and within minutes, all of them had disappeared. When he was hanging on the Cross, only one of the eleven apostles was mentioned as being there.

Jesus' teachings were harsh to the ears of the multitudes that came out of curiosity to see the man that was healing the sick, feeding those that were hungry, and working miracles. They were not looking for charter membership in a group whose leader undauntedly told them that it would be costly to follow him.

John the Baptist asked of his listeners, "Who gave you warning to flee from the coming wrath?" This soul-searching warning led John's hearers to ask him, "What shall we do?" The answer from John was repentance, which was to come from the sincerity of their hearts. John was preparing the way for the one whose "shoelaces he was not worthy to tie." When Jesus is preached today, the Holy Spirit of God brings conviction to the hearts of the unsaved to receive Jesus, just as John the Baptist prepared his listeners for the coming of Jesus Christ.

John the Baptist referred to his generation of listeners as "a brood of vipers." In today's Christianity, unbelievers live in what some believe is a more sophisticated society. Who in today's pulpits call their listeners to repentance in the way that John did? Instead of getting to the very soul of those who attend church, ministers primarily preach the church and its programs.

Jesus' teachings and requirement that "those who are not willing to leave home and family for my sake are not fit for the Kingdom of God" were unpleasant words to his hearers. Most that heard these requirements discovered that they had other plans, and began to make excuses: "first let me go and bury my father, and then I will come and follow you." For them, there were far more important present-day plans than following the one who claimed that he "was the Son of Man."

Jesus became even more explicit: "once a person has put his hands to the plow, and looks back, he is not fit for the Kingdom." Does the preaching of John and Jesus sound like the preaching that you are hearing in churches today? How many of today's listeners would come back the following Sunday to listen to such prerequisites for membership into His Kingdom? God wants to be number one, requiring that He be worshipped and adored.

The chosen twelve apostles became an intimate part of the inner circle of Jesus. Existing in the lives of these apostles were jealousy and rivalry, and not one of them became perfect. Some wanted to become number one. They became his cabinet and carried on their shoulders different functions and responsibilities within the group. One can only surmise that committee meetings were held to a minimum after Jesus had given them directions.

JESUS' TEACHINGS LEAD TO AN EXODUS

As Jesus and the disciples went about the countryside, they attracted followers. One day while teaching in the synagogue in Capernaum, Jesus made some very strong statements about himself. "Many of his disciples, not the twelve, on hearing what Jesus had said, remarked: 'This is a very difficult teaching, and who can accept it?'" Many that were seeking to become disciples turned back and no longer followed Jesus.

Those that left, left Jesus for good, and didn't continue to taint the others with their unbelief and unwillingness to follow the teachings of Jesus. Judas Iscariot remained within the movement for the same reason that today's self-proclaiming Christians remain. Unbelievers have their own purposes and motives for staying within the pews of a local church.

Again, the number one motivation for claiming Christianity by those who are without Christ is heaven, believing that churchgoing and membership will be the ticket.

Jesus' reaction to this exodus was: "This is why I told you that not one can come to me unless the Father has enabled him." Jesus had known from the beginning that there would be unbelievers and so-called followers. Jesus, being knowledgeable of Old Testament prophecies, was keenly aware that one within the twelve would betray him to the religious leaders of that day.

Jesus, upon seeing his followers leave, said to the twelve, "Do you want to leave too?" This was an avenue for Judas and any of the others to leave, but Judas, being an opportunist, chose to remain in the confines of this small group. Peter, hearing the question posed by Jesus, asked him where they would go if they left.

Peter reaffirmed his faith in Jesus by proclaiming that Jesus was God's Holy One. Peter recognized that Jesus was the one that had the words of eternal life. The faith that Peter proclaimed was the kind of faith that brought God's Kingdom to "those that would confess with their mouths the Lord Jesus, and believe in their hearts that God had raised him from the dead."

MILLIONS WITHIN CHURCHES DON'T REALIZE THEIR LOSTNESS

Having been in the presence of Jesus for at least three years, one would conclude that Judas would have eventually come to a saving knowledge of the Lord. However, Judas' heart was hardened to the teaching of Jesus. In today's Christianity, one would also reason that the unsaved, who have been sitting for years in the pews of churches in various denominations, would eventually be saved. It doesn't happen that way! It is only when the Spirit of the Living God is drawing people to the Cross that the unsaved can come to God.

A goodly number of those who are unsaved don't know that they are lost. Many of them have hearts that have been hardened to the wooing of the Holy Spirit. Over the years, they have been taught to believe that it's all about church-going, and when they remain faithful in attendance, that everything is alright between them and the Lord.

Parents for ages have taught their children that it is a sin to fail to go to church on Sunday or whatever day of the week their beliefs would cause them to attend. Having been taught this by parents, these same children, who are now adults and parents, are teaching their children the same.

Children have been known to awaken on Sunday mornings and say: "I just don't think that I can make it today! I just don't feel well!"

"Well, if you're not able to go to church, then you are not going to go out this afternoon," becomes the response of parents. In essence, what children hear is this: "you can expect punishment when you don't go to church or you can get rewarded when you do."

Church attendance is taught from day one by many parents as the primary reason for going to church. After becoming adults, some of these children, being able to make their own decisions, no longer go to church. Do they claim to be Christians? Of course they do! And these children, having now become adults, are teaching their children the philosophy that they were taught by their parents.

I have witnessed parents in their house-robes driving to church with their children, dropping them off, and returning home. What a witness this is to their children! I suppose if these children should question their parents as to why it was so important for them to go and not the parents, the answer would be, "I know everything that I need to know about the Bible." Their graduate degree had already been attained.

Judas might have felt the same way about getting up day after day to follow Jesus. "We keep on doing the same old routine every day, and not much is happening," could have been his thoughts.

Judas had monetary thoughts that far outweighed his spiritual needs. Thirty pieces of silver became far more attractive to Judas than walking around the countryside with a godly man who was requiring so much of him and the other disciples. The thirty pieces of silver was far more money than was presently in the treasury pouch that he was carrying. The physical and monetary needs for most of the churchgoing public will always outweigh their spiritual needs. Infiltrators come to church neither to have a spiritual encounter nor to be awakened to the fact that they are in need of one.

Judas could have reasoned that if Jesus were turned over to the authorities, this might provoke Jesus to bring in the "kingdom" that he had been preaching about. Judas could later justify his actions to Jesus by saying that he had done it for Jesus' good. Judas had to take matters into his own hands. If it failed to get Jesus to act, Judas knew that Jesus would be forgiving. The way that Jesus was going about it was taking too long, and it appeared that the movement was going nowhere. While the motives of Judas are strictly speculative, he was not a follower of the Lord Jesus.

Judas was an unbelieving pretender from the beginning. He had been chosen by Jesus to become one of his disciples, and he went along for the ride. Persons are invited to join the church today, and can easily get their names entered on the rolls of churches—not even having to pay an initiation fee. What better offer can one get than that? One can walk to the front of the church, take the minister or someone else by the hand, and say, "I want to join your church and become a member."

That walk down the aisle for some may be a difficult thing to do. If one is a very shy person, and just can't make that walk before so many people, one can call ahead to some ministers during the week, explain the dilemma, and ask to be received without the walk. How easy it is to become a member of a Christian body! Today, in some churches, some chat with the minister before the service, because an invitation to join might not be given at the conclusion of the service.

"How do you come?" might be one of the questions asked by the minister. The questions now depend on what the church has established for the reception of new members. Some churches require more than others. For example, if you are walking the aisle of a Baptist church, one of the requirements is for baptism or water immersion.

The same denomination or others might ask, "Do you believe in God?" The response could be: "Sure, I believe that, and I have believed that all of my life. My parents were God-fearing people."

That's the routine. Some ministers have been known to ask about "repentance" and "sincerity" of heart, and if you are "saved." Denominations and church rolls are exploding with members who are unsaved. Judas became an infiltrator among the twelve, and he stuck in there for three years or more. Some unbelievers, whose names are among born-again believers, have hung on for years. They have had their children baptized in the church, married in the church, and been buried in the church. This is what Christianity is for them—having someone around for these amenities.

JUDAS' BETRAYAL

Judas sold out to the chief priests and religious leaders for thirty pieces of silver. Feeling some remorse over the exploding events, Judas went back to them, trying to return the coins. No one wanted anything to do with "blood money." Judas didn't want the coins, nor did the priests want them.

The money ended up being used to purchase a piece of land for a potter's field.

Judas hung himself. The one who had walked, talked, fellowshipped, and heard the teachings of Jesus was never converted. That is the way that it is in denominations and churches today. Unbelievers come; they mingle; they talk, listen, eat food together, and participate in programs; yet there is no giving of heart and soul to the Master. They will continue to remain until the "sheep are separated from the goats."

Regardless of what is being said today about a "Judas Gospel," and Jesus asking Judas to betray him, it can only be negated to the trash dumps of our minds. Letters that come out of the third century are unable to contradict the writers that were there centuries before and were available for untruths to be challenged by first century witnesses. A Judas gospel is strictly speculative brainwashing by sensationalists vying for present day monetary benefits that far exceed thirty pieces of silver.

MEDITATION

A TRIP BACK IN TIME

The next trip that the two of us took was to the courtyards of the temple in Jerusalem where we came upon a very unpleasant and unruly scene. Pharisees with some teachers of the law came with a woman in tow and headed for the courtyards where they had heard that Jesus was teaching. After finding Jesus, the woman was made to stand in the middle of the group. An appointed spokesman had a question for Jesus:

"Teacher, this woman was caught in the act of adultery. In the Law, Moses commanded us to stone such women. Now what do you say?"

My friend and I looked at each other and were amazed at what was happening. It was then that I turned to my friend and said, "I've read somewhere in Moses Law that both the man and the woman caught in adultery were to be stoned. Where is the man, if the woman was caught in the act?"

"That's a good question," he murmured.

Someone close by, and hearing our remarks said, "I wouldn't worry too much about that for it isn't the woman who is on trial here, but Jesus. They are trying to set a trap, and to find fault with him."

Not bothering to answer the question asked, Jesus bent down and with his finger began writing on the ground. My friend and I moved a little closer to see what he was writing. There was a lot of chattering within the group of religious leaders as they continued their questioning of Jesus.

Jesus, stopping his writing, straightened up and said, "If anyone of you is without sin, let him be the first to throw a stone at her." Having said this, he again stooped down and continued his writing in the sand. It was at that moment that the questions stopped, and then one by one, the oldest to the youngest, left the scene.

My friend and I were now able to get closer to Jesus and the woman as Jesus straightened up, and for the first time, he looked directly into the eyes of the woman.

"Woman, where are they? Has no one condemned you?"

"No one, sir," she said.

With compassion and forgiveness, Jesus said, "Then neither do I condemn you." Go and leave your life of sin."

As all of them left, my friend and I went to see what Jesus had written on the ground. His words were written in a language that was unfamiliar to us. But, there at the end, written in English, were the names of my friend and me.

—derived from John 8:1-11.

CHAPTER ELEVEN

CIRCUMCISED, CHRISTENED, AND CONFIRMED

.... ."Let the little children come to me, and do not hinder them, for the kingdom of God belongs to such as these." Mark 10:14b

CHURCHES DON'T MAKE CHRISTIANS

Christians are not made by being circumcised, christened, or confirmed. Christians are born spiritually from above by the Heavenly Father and not by human means. The acts or rituals of being circumcised, christened, and confirmed are decisions usually made by parents for their children. Because of these rites, some people get the impression that a "'prerequisite'" has been met, and the recipient has become a Christian.

Adolescents, when reaching certain ages, often confirm their Christian faith in some denominations. Confirmation classes are scheduled for these young adolescents who may have been christened as children. Thus, the confirming of one's faith becomes a matter routinely determined by the church and usually the parents of these young adolescents.

Some denominational churches believe that those who have been christened as babies and those who are attending church, having now reached a certain age, are old enough to confirm their faith. These young adolescents need to confirm and examine their faith in Jesus Christ, but no one should be making a decision for them about when they are to accept Christ. For the adolescents it should be a sincere personal heartfelt decision made only by them, and not by a parent, minister, or the church. No denomination or church can make Christians.

When a child is sprinkled, usually soon after birth, it is the parents making the decisions for the child. Some parents want to dedicate their children to the Lord and ask that they be christened.

Babies and very young children are not capable of making the decision to accept Jesus as their Savior until they have reached some degree of maturity or accountability, and the recognition on their part that they are sinners. This happens when a child is able to recognize that there is sin in his or her life, and that it isn't against their parents, but personally between him or herself and God. Salvation through repentance and faith in Jesus Christ comes through the personal decision by an individual who has been given a free will to choose or reject.

Many people in the United States go to the polls and register to vote during local, state, and national elections. There are certain requirements that a person has to meet in order to qualify as a registered voter. Those whose names are added to the register have met all of the requirements that have been established by state and federal laws. Many of those whose names are on voting registers will never exercise their rights to vote. The privilege of voting was made available, but they didn't go beyond the signing-up process.

So it is with many of the children who are baptized, christened, and confirmed. Some never get beyond the rituals afforded them, and will never come to the saving knowledge of having a personal relationship with the Lord Jesus Christ. They have been led to believe, and will reason later, that what has been done for them is all that is necessary in claiming the name of a Christian.

Some eighty-five percent of Americans make claims to following a Christian faith, according to recent surveys. Considering that there are three hundred million Americans, there are two hundred fifty-five million Americans "leaning" toward Christianity. These are staggering figures! Churches could not hold such numbers on any given day of worship. Christians, however, are not made by "following and leaning" toward a belief in Christianity.

It is my contention that less than thirty percent of Americans from this humungous number of self-leaning Christians have had a personal encounter with the Lord Jesus, committed their lives to Him, and are following his teachings. How would an estimated figure of only seventy-six million Americans being born-again believers sound? Today's lifestyles and secularism prove these figures to more accurately gauge Christianity in America. This certainly agrees with Biblical teachings that only a few will be saved.

Delving a little further, there are over two billion people in the world that claim or lean toward Christianity as their faith. The majority of these don't know the meaning or definition of what a Christian is, and how to be in that category. To validate this, one has only to do his or her own personal random sampling of asking ten or more people: "What makes you think that you are a Christian?" Listen carefully to the responses and decide if they meet with the statement by Jesus when he said, "I am the way, the truth and the life."

Willie Nelson, in a recent interview with Time magazine, had this to say about his beliefs: "I believe that all roads lead to the same place. We're taking different ways to get there, but we all end up in the same place." This was in answer to the comment made during the interview about his Methodist roots. Mr. Nelson went further to say, "May the God of your choice bless you. That's the main thoughts that I have about life."

I would suppose that he was not speaking of a cemetery, but of a heavenly home. Millions of Americans hold to the philosophy that there are many roads that lead to heaven. But these philosophies are manmade beliefs and not the teachings of the Scriptures.

A MISUNDERSTANDING OF THE WORD "CHRISTIAN"

As a thirteen-year-old boy, standing on a street corner waiting for a bus in Atlanta, Georgia, I was asked if I were a Christian. The Salvation Army was across the street in front of a drug store, playing their musical instruments. One of its members approached and asked the question: "Are you a Christian?" I was embarrassed and didn't really know how to answer, because I was not sure what a 'Christian' was. The bus rescued me from having to answer that question.

It was, however, a question that remained with me, and would bother me for the rest of the night. Early the next morning, I approached my mother with the question, "Am I a Christian?" She answered in the affirmative, and may have made the remark that we lived in America, and surely I wasn't a heathen. It wasn't until years later that I asked Jesus to come into my life and to save me from my sins.

There are multitudes of Christian claimers throughout the world who are like that thirteen-year-old boy, for they are in doubt about what a Christian is, and have never had a personal encounter with Jesus. They know very little about the teachings of the Bible, and have never been saved. As Jesus said to Nicodemus, "you must be born again."

Why do so many people believe that they are Christians, when in essence they don't understand or practice Christianity? There are many answers to that question, and the answers will vary according to a previous teaching or an understanding that they received from their parents, husband, wife, friends, church, and, yes, even a pastor or priest.

In finding answers to why so many self-proclaiming churchgoers are lost and without God, reasons will vary according to upbringing; what peers believe; rubbing elbows with associates; daily contacts with others; and church teachings. Today's populace has very little knowledge about the Bible and its teachings. The Bible is a best seller that has been scarcely read by the masses.

THE MISUNDERSTANDING ABOUT RITES WITHIN CHURCHES

One thing that confuses some into believing that they are Christians is the act of "christening or baptizing" in some churches. In some churches there is the desire and request of parents to having their babies christened at a very early age. Churchgoing parents bring their newborns to church to have them sprinkled or dedicated to the Lord.

I can see nothing wrong with having a child baptized or christened when it is explained to the parents and congregation that the child is being dedicated to the Lord and that the sprinkling is not Christian baptism. In fact, I love this ritual of bringing our children to the Lord. The parents and the congregation are agreeing to bring the child up in the Christian faith. The reason behind this ceremony should in later years be explained to the child so that he or she will understand what has been done, and that a person is not Christianized by these rites.

HANNAH'S GIFT TO THE LORD

It is recorded in the Old Testament that a woman went with her husband to worship and offer sacrifices to the Lord at a temple near the city of Shiloh. She was unable to have children, and this deeply troubled her. She was sitting outside the temple, crying and praying deep within her heart about the situation. In her prayer the woman had made a vow to God that if He would give her a son that she would give him back to the Lord all the days of his life. She, being childless, believed that she had not fulfilled her wifely duty to her husband.

The priest, seeing the woman's condition, believed that the woman was drunk. He could see the woman crying and even though her lips were moving, her voice was not being heard.

"How long will you keep on getting drunk?" the priest asked her. "Get rid of your wine."

The woman explained to the priest that she had not been drinking, but that she was a woman in deep distress and troubled. Out of her anguish and grief, she told the priest that she was praying to the Lord for relief. It was then that he told the woman to go in peace and may the Lord grant to her what she had asked of Him.

The Lord heard the woman's petition and granted what she had asked. Later she became the mother of a son. Her vow had been that she would give him to the Lord, and after her son was weaned, she took him to the temple and gave him to the priest. The child grew up in the temple under the watchful eye of the priest and carried out the duties that were assigned to him. Even though he had been dedicated and given to the Lord as a baby by his mother, the young child, upon reaching accountability, would have to exercise his own faith in God and would have to experience God's calling.

It was during the night a few years later that God's call came to the boy who had been named Samuel. God called, but Samuel thought that it was the voice of the priest. Samuel ran to the priest, only to find that he was not the one that had called him. It was only at the third calling by God on the same night, that the priest told Samuel that it was God that was calling him, and that if he called again to say, "Speak Lord, for your servant is listening."

Samuel had been raised and worked in the temple, but he still did not "know" the Lord and the word of the Lord had not been revealed to him. So it is with a baby or child who is christened, dedicated, baptized, or taken to church. The decision to christen and to baptize is a choice made by a parent or another and is not a decision that the child is able to make. The Bible is explicit in expressing the need for a personal decision. The decision to become a Christian is one that is made by repentance, faith, and personal choice.

THE SIGNIFICANCE OF RITES WITHIN CHURCHES

Again, I find no fault with baptism or christening as long as the recipients are not misled into believing that they have become Christians by being exposed to this ritual. The parents, when having their children christened, dedicated, or baptized, should be saying to the church that they are going to teach their children the precepts of Christianity, promising to do so by leading a godly life before them. Teaching is to begin in the home.

The church's congregation where these rites are being offered says that they, too, are taking these children under their watchful care. When the children who have been dedicated or christened realize that they are sinners, the need for repentance, confession, and acceptance of the Lord Jesus should become real to them. Some of those who are christened will go through life and will never make that personal decision, thinking and believing that they are Christians and that no further decision is necessary on their part.

In later years, one of these persons who have been baptized, christened, or dedicated at an early age may be asked the question: "Are you a Christian?" They might readily answer, "Yes, I am," and tell you that they have been christened or baptized.

Recently, my daughter gave birth to her first child, a boy. When I was afforded the opportunity to hold him in my arms for the first time, it was under my breath, not meaning for others to hear, that I asked God to bless him. It was then that I asked the Lord to use him, dedicating him to the Lord. No one in that hospital room knew that I had made that prayer request to God. It was between God and me, and I knew that God was aware of my thoughts and desire. The grandson in my arms was not aware of my praying to God, and had no idea of what I was asking of God. My grandson will have to make his own decision about Jesus when he reaches the age of accountability.

A few hours later my grandson was circumcised and it had no Christian significance. Circumcising male infants has become a custom today in America, mainly for health reasons.

The circumcision that my grandson experienced had nothing to do with the covenant that God made with Abraham that all male children were to be circumcised on the eighth day after birth. The circumcision that took place with Abraham and his descendants was to be a sign of the covenant that existed between Abraham and the Lord God.

The baby Jesus was circumcised on the eighth day, and as instructed by the angel, was given his name. This was a custom of the Jews. Circumcision was to symbolize their direct relationship to God and His covenant and was to show their distinct separation from Gentiles.

One month after the birth of a male child during Biblical times, the child was presented to the Lord by the parents, who acknowledged that God was the giver of life. It was a "redeeming back" process by the parents of male children, who then made an offering to God. The parents went through these Mosaic teachings of keeping the law. Thus, it was the parents making the decisions for their offspring.

We can appreciate a mother and father bringing a child to the altar, because they are coming with gratitude in their hearts for God's blessings for this gift of life. It is a scene that invites rejoicing and praise to the Almighty from the parents, and from those who are witnessing a very special event in the life of the child and the church.

We should not read into these rites something that is not intended. Our prayer should be that the significance of the event will be later expressed by the recipient in an act of acceptance and faith in Jesus Christ.

MEDITATION

A TRIP BACK IN TIME

The sun was beginning to rise over the Sea of Tiberias as boats were returning to shore with their catches. Fishermen, oftentimes exhausted from their night's labor, would clean their nets, get ready to eat, and then go off to bed.

My friend and I, tired from our travel, were looking forward to this time on the coast—to hearing the clanging of bells and the shrieks of the seagulls and watching as boats unloaded their catch for the market. Serenity washed away our weariness as we stood by the sea watching the waves as they went back and forth sweeping and cleansing the shore. We removed our sandals to feel the waves as they sought a haven between our toes.

It appeared that some of these fishermen had made arrangements in advance for their morning meal. For off in an isolated place on the beach was a lone individual, firing up coals, getting ready to cook what would be brought to him. The one preparing the fire must have grown impatient, and not wanting to waste his time should his friends be returning without fish, called out to those on the boat:

"Friends, haven't you any fish?"

The one preparing the coals for cooking must have personally known the seven fishermen on the boat. It could have been by the way that they moved or even a shrug of their shoulders which told him that they were discouraged and downtrodden.

"No!" they called back.

The lone voice from the beach called back to them saying, "Throw your net on the right side of the boat and you will find some."

Under their breath, some of them were probably murmuring, "What does he know about it?"

They didn't question his suggestion. There must have been something about that voice, like a command, that prompted them to throw their net over the starboard side of the boat. All seven of them were unable to haul into the boat the one hundred fifty-three large fish that they would later count and take out of the net.

We heard one of them struggling with the net shout out to another, "It is the Lord!"

Upon hearing, "It is the Lord," one of the fishermen in haste and with added enthusiasm, wrapped his outer garment around himself and jumped into the water, while the others remained with the boat. After securing the boat, all of them walked to where the fire had been prepared.

The one preparing the coals said to the seven, "Bring some of the fish that you have just caught."

Hurriedly, they went back to the boat to drag the net ashore.

"Come and have breakfast," said the morning chef.

None of the seven asked him, "Who are you?" for they knew that it was their resurrected Lord.

Jesus took some bread and gave it to them. He then did the same with the fish.

My friend and I stayed at a distance and didn't enter into this intimate, reconciliatory meeting with Jesus, Simon Peter, Thomas, Nathanael, James, John, and two other disciples, whom we were unable to identify. Undoubtedly, they had gone back to their old ways. And yes, they were discouraged, depressed, and lost without Jesus to give them directions for the future.

This meeting between Jesus and seven of his disciples became holy ground that my friend and I dare not tread on.

As we turned to walk away, my friend and I talked about how futile one's work can be without the Lord's direction.

My friend turned to me and said, "They toiled all night without a fish, and in a very brief moment, Jesus called out to them, 'Throw your net on the right side of the boat.'"

"Yes," I responded. "Would you and I, being as tired as they, put our nets back into the water?"

—derived from John 21:1-14.

CHAPTER TWELVE

CHURCHGOING ADDICTIONS

". . . zeal for your house consumes me," Psalm 69:9a

Recently I conducted a simple non-professional survey among a few churchgoers in order to get a better understanding of why they, as well as others, go to church. Some of those surveyed came up with their own reasons, but with few exceptions to those that were already in my thoughts. This is not an all-inclusive list. The reasons given in this survey are not new ones, because some reasons for going to church become transparent in the lives of churchgoers by their actions, deeds, and beliefs. This simple survey revealed that there are positives as well as negatives for church attendance.

THE APPEASISTS: People go to church to appease others. Sometimes it is difficult to turn down an invitation to attend church with a wife, husband, friend, relative, boyfriend, girlfriend, or a coworker, especially if the invitation to attend is of a consistent nature. Some people appease to please others and to be accepted. The invitee may come to like the service that is offered and become a regular participant, sometimes joining and remaining in the status of unbeliever or becoming a born-again believer.

THE ASSEMBLISTS: Born-again believers go to church to worship and fellowship with people who feel the same way about the Lord as they do. The Lord intended that we assemble together with other believers: "Let us not give up meeting together as some are in the habit of doing, but let us encourage one another, and all the more as you see the Day approaching."

Some Assemblists go because they are lonely and in need of fellowship with others who are living under circumstances similar to their own. Within the walls of any church setting there are individuals who are widowed, divorced, separated, unemployed, and with lost friendships. They know burdens can be lifted through sharing experiences by assembling with those living or having lived with similar experiences.

THE CONDITIONISTS: Parents go to church because they want their children to be morally conditioned to the things that they themselves were exposed to as a child. Due to this conditioning by their parents, they, too, recognize the need to get their children some 'religious' training. Parents with very little knowledge of the Scriptures are not spiritually equipped to provide Biblical training, so they send or go with them to church to be 'conditioned' and exposed to the faith.

THE CONFESSIONISTS: Some feel a need to atone for their sinful thoughts and actions during the week. There exists a heartfelt need for forgiveness from their sinfulness. There always will be an immediate and persistent need of those who are saved to confess their sins before the Lord.

THE CONNECTIONISTS: True believers go to church to connect and to praise God, seeking a spiritual blessing of renewal. Unbelievers primarily go to make a connection with others. The unsaved are unable to connect spiritually with God because the Holy Spirit of God is not living within them. The unbelievers leave in the same condition as when they arrived.

THE FISHERISTS: People go to church to fish for a friend or a mate. If a person is looking for someone, the best possibilities, supposedly, are within the confines of a church. Those having their names on church roles are believed to be Christians, and believers are not to be yoked together in marriage with unbelievers. There are those in churches who are single, divorced, or widowed. The belief remains that the church is a safe haven when fishing for a mate with the same denominational background.

THE FOLLOWISTS: Some attend church because they are preacher-followers. It is appalling that some churchgoing people are preacher-led or preacher-followers. Some are so entwined with a former pastor that they will go often to hear him preach on a new church field. There are ministers who encourage this through their efforts to continue their relationships with former parishioners.

It is regretful that some ministers cater to certain people within their congregations. Some pastors seek out those who will cater to them and with whom they feel more comfortable. Ministers soon become aware of those that they have to please the most, and will make attempts to stay on good terms. These persons become a sounding board to ministers who are willing to cater to their whims.

THE MEDITATIONISTS: Believers look for quiet moments to meditate and connect with God. Peace, comfort, and solitude are found in a sanctuary where God's presence seems to be more real. Unbelievers can even be caught up in the serenity and tranquility that can be found inside a church. There are trials, temptations, afflictions, and illnesses in one's journey from birth until death. Society is full of hurting people, and no community is immune. When the walls are tumbling down and the foundations are crumbling, some seek the quietness of a church to meditate.

THE NEEDISTS: There will always be the need for believers to attend church, for it is there that they not only worship their Creator, but hear and study His Word. There is a need on the part of believers to hear and share in the Word of God. They come to hear God's message be proclaimed and to partake of the spiritual food that they are seeking. Just as an automobile is in need of servicing every so often, so does Christians need to be recharged by hearing and participating in the sharing of God's Word.

In the human soul there is an on-going need to learn more about the Bible under a Spirit-led leader. Many adults, especially those whom have "grown-up" in the church, believe they know already what they need to know about the Bible. Those holding such beliefs are not allowing God to speak to them through the pages of the written Word. The Bible should be read daily to feed the need for things other than the material.

THE OPPORTUNISTS: It is obvious and undeniable that some go to church for business contacts. I once attended a church where the pastor, upon receiving new members into the church, gave the places of employment for the new members. Jokingly, the pastor mentioned that to each new member he gave a one-time advertisement for their occupation or vocation.

Some church members openly hand out their business cards or make other members aware of their livelihood. This appears to be prevalent among some salespersons and the most undeniable reason why some of them may be going to church. Churchgoing is the best non-paid advertisement that a person can receive.

Christian brothers and sisters should do business with each other, providing they are competitive with similar businesses. It is not difficult to distinguish some believers from unbelievers when at church. Those who are members of a church for the sole reason of making business contacts are usually noticeable.

THE PARTICIPATIONISTS: People go to church to participate in the various organizations such as choirs, youth activities, women's and men's organizations, and other functions. Churchgoers like to participate with those having the same beliefs, purposes, talents, and goals. It's a marvelous way to display God-given talent, rub elbows with church members, attain some degree of recognition, and to grow spiritually.

THE PREDECESSORISTS: People go to church because that is what they have been taught by their predecessors— usually parents or grandparents. They have become traditionalists, and going to church has become a way of life.

Children, after leaving the nest and living in the same community, often attend the same church regardless of beliefs, strictly because their ancestors attended. A new minister, whom they might disagree with because of personality or theology, is often endured until another one is called or appointed. They will not break with tradition and will not let go of sentimentalism. They often refer to the church as "my church."

THE REGENERATIONISTS: People go to church because it makes them feel good. "It is good to be in the House of the Lord." For some, "it's the pause that refreshes." Regeneration comes from being refreshed and renewed by God.

The apostle Peter said to Jesus: "Lord, it is good for us to be here. If you wish, I will put up three shelters—one for you, one for Moses, and one for Elijah."

God doesn't deny to the believer that regenerated feeling that comes from being in His house. The feeling of regeneration that comes to the unbeliever is being absent and apart from the secular world for a few moments. Peter felt refreshed in the presence of John and James, and apart from the world, when Jesus was transfigured before them. Believers return to secular work feeling "charged" by having been in a worshipful atmosphere. Unbelievers return feeling "good" about having attended church.

THE RESTORATIONISTS: Believers go to church to get restored. They feel the emptiness within and want to be filled. The physical aspects of the past week have not produced satisfaction and contentment, and they feel drained of all spiritual aspects.

Sunday morning and Sunday night services are not enough for some, and they go back on Wednesday or during the week to get restored. There's a necessity on the part of the Christian to stay as close to the Lord as possible. Believers are in constant need of this restoration of spirit.

THE SECURITYISTS: Some go to church because they are in need of a minister to perform weddings, visit them when sick, and to eulogize them at death. Some plan in advance to have a minister available for happy and sorrowful events. There is security in having a minister available to perform important functions and to offer solace.

Some churches have burial grounds, and provide burial spaces without charge to members. Ministers are put in awkward positions when asked to perform the eulogy for a deceased member that is an unknown to them. In any church there are members who have not attended church for years. The information from the "dash" in between birth and death has to be gathered from friends and family. Hearsay information is relied upon when the officiating person knows little about the deceased, for some "died" on the church rolls years before.

THE SOCIALIZERISTS: People go to engage in social activities, believing that the church is a good place to socialize. Many organizations within the church family lend themselves to social activities. These church functions offer many opportunities to socialize for the youths, adults, and the elderly. God is to be glorified in all of these activities.

THE SUPERFICIALISTS: Some churchgoers attend church so they can appear good to other people. With over 2.1 billion people worldwide claiming to be Christians, some don't want to be an outsider looking in. Their religious tendencies are superficial in nature. Millions want to be card-holding church members so they can relate to others who are claiming the same affiliation.

THE SUPERSTITIONISTS: Many go to church because of superstition or religious guilt. Some go because they feel that something bad might happen to them or feeling a sense of guilt should they not go. When bad luck befalls them it is often blamed on their failure to attend church, feeling that God has brought a dilemma upon them. "I've got to start going again to church," some will proclaim.

Christianity is not about luck, nor is it about superstition. God does not punish people for not going to church, but will allow and permit things to happen when His people are disobedient. Some hold to beliefs that if they don't tithe or submit an offering, that God is going to get it through some breakdown of an appliance or an automobile, or by other means.

There are varied reasons why people attend church, whether occasionally or to be there when the doors are opened. Some politicians never darken church doors until they run for an elective office. There is some feeling in America, among churchgoing people, that a person seeking an elective office should be a member of a church or have some 'religious' beliefs. Politicians court the churchgoing public to win their vote.

To maintain some degree of brevity about why people go to church, a slight mention will be made about those who go to show off a stunning outfit; those who attend only two services a year, namely Easter and Christmas; those who attend when it is convenient; those who attend before, during, and after a crisis; and those parents and grandparents who go to see their children participate in a production or play.

After all these classifications about why people go to church—what is the primary and foremost reason for going to church? Is it not to worship the Lord God? Believers go to church to praise, honor, and worship our Creator. That is what churchgoing is about. The words that are spoken inside the sanctuary are to be words of praise directed to God. The hymns or songs that are sung, are meant for his 'ears' and not ours.

I was glad when they said unto me, "Let us go into the House of the Lord."

MEDITATION

A TRIP BACK IN TIME

Having watched the breakfast meal of bread and fish that Jesus prepared for seven of his disciples, we now began to prepare for our departure back to the twenty-first century.

It was then that my friend said, "Haven't we missed something here? Surely, Jesus didn't come to just cook breakfast for them? There is no doubt that He appeared to let them know that he is alive, but shouldn't we stay and see what is yet to come?"

"You're right," I said. "Certainly we don't want to intrude, but let's stay around to see what Jesus will talk with them about."

Immediately after the meal, Jesus turned to the oldest one in the group, and addressing him by name, asked: "Simon, son of John, do you love me more than these?" It appeared that Jesus was asking him if he loved him with an unconditional type of love and with a love that seeks nothing in return.

"Yes!" the man responded. "You know that I love you because you are my friend."

"Feed my lambs," said Jesus.

An unbearable silence enveloped the group of disciples as they lowered their heads and shuffled their sandals in the sand. Was Jesus talking to Simon about them, the boat, the fishing, when he said, "more than these?" Jesus interrupted their thoughts to ask again:

"Simon, son of John, do you truly love me with a God-given love?" asked Jesus.

The air became thick, the man's breathing became heavier, and with a look of embarrassment, he answered:

"Yes, Lord, you know that I love you because you are my friend."

Jesus said, "Take care of my sheep."

Again, the one who had answered in the affirmative to the questioning of Jesus was asked for the third time: "Simon, son of John do you love me?" "Are you even my friend?"

"Lord, you know all things; you know that I love you. You are my friend." said the man.

"Feed my sheep," said Jesus.

The hurt was now showing in the face of the man that we had now come to know as Simon Peter. His thoughts had to be about the night that Jesus was arrested. He and John had followed the arresting party from a distance, and then having gone into the courtyard, had those around the fire accuse him of being one of Jesus' disciples.

Three times he was asked about his relationship with Jesus, and each time he had denied knowing him. The rooster crowed and Jesus had turned and looked at him. He left the courtyard and the warmness of the fire, to wash away his denials with heartfelt tears.

Everything was now being made right between Peter and Jesus, for Jesus had come to offer his reassurance and forgiveness to Peter. Familiar words were being heard by the group as Jesus said, "follow me."

Never again would there be another denial by Peter of Jesus. Peter would continue to follow Jesus until history records that he was crucified upside down on a cross.

It had been a somber moment for my friend and me, for we had witnessed a renewal of commitments and the putting of priorities in their proper order.

We, too, had experienced God's love and forgiveness, early in the morning on a shore by the sea, where fishing for fish would be forgotten.

— derived from John 21:15-19.

CHAPTER THIRTEEN

LOVE FOR THE CHURCH

"No one can serve two masters. Either he will hate the one and love the other, or he will be devoted to the one and despise the other . . . ." Matt. 6:24a

THE "USED-TO-ERS"

Often heard among churchgoing adults is talk of their being carried to church by their parents, and being made to go or suffer the consequences. No argument is raised by me about these parents requiring their children to attend church, since a person can hear in some churches Jesus being preached, a call to repentance, and being saved.

Two lifestyles are now being lived by some of these parent-conditioned, made-to-go churchgoers, the one lived for a few hours on Sunday, versus the one lived during the week. Walking down the church aisle and claiming to know Jesus in order to gain membership has become a routine for adolescents after attending for years with parents.

In some denominations, children are confirmed after reaching a certain age. They then become church members after confirmation classes, which may lead them to believe that they are now Christians. Their faith is confirmed, but that doesn't mean that they have had a conversion experience. Conversion to Christianity is a matter of the heart and is not based on church rites. The Holy Spirit does the convincing and brings conversion to those who are in true repentance and acceptance by faith of Jesus as their Savior.

David Brooks, of the New York Times, quoted Harold Ford, a Tennessee Democrat seeking a United States Senate seat in 2006 as saying, ". . . We didn't have any choice. Where I grew up, when you awakened on Sunday, you went to church. I learned the faith thing the old fashioned way." Mr. Ford is saying that he "learned the faith thing," or about churchgoing, from family. Churchgoing is emphasized instead of a conversion experience.

Many "learn the faith thing" by becoming habitual churchgoers, hearing often the message of Christ being preached, but never coming to a state of repentance and personal acceptance of Jesus. Hearing the message of Christ repeatedly without experiencing repentance, produces calloused hearts and dull ears. After a while, for the made-to-go unbeliever, there becomes no heartfelt need to respond to repentance and faith. The churchgoer, whether through ignorance of the Bible or out of habitual attendance, comes to believe that churchgoing has brought Christianity. These are the ones who are lost and don't know it.

At eleven o'clock on a Sunday morning in some churches, the pastor enters from the front of the church, closely followed by a number of deacons. In some churches the deacons might sit in the pews with their wives and children. It doesn't matter how they enter or where they sit. What's important is that many of these leaders are among the lost and have become only churchgoers by not having had a personal relationship with Jesus.

From the pews, parishioners view their leaders as good outstanding men in the community. They have come up through the ranks, and are the "pillars" of the church.

These leaders have been elected by a congregational vote as men worthy of respect: "not indulging in much wine, not pursuing or having been involved in any dishonest gains, being in control of their household, and are husbands of only one wife." They have met all of the requirements set forth in the Bible for the selection of leaders, and have been examined by a group of their peers.

Church members consider deacons, elders, or their leaders to be dedicated men. They are there when the church doors are opened. While others are sleeping, some arrive early to turn on air conditioners or the heat, preparing in advance a comfortable atmosphere for parishioners and guests. They are "good" men according to worldly standards, but those who have dealings with them away from the church will know by their actions whether these leaders are true believers in the Lord Jesus Christ. Some have been "conditioned" to being good men by their ancestors, becoming more consistent churchgoers. Some of these men have placed their emphasis on churchgoing and doing good, rather than on Christ.

By no means am I saying that chosen leaders of the church are not good outstanding men. Many of them are totally committed to the teachings of the Bible and to doing good works, while endeavoring to live the life of Christian witnesses. Some of them, just like Judas, have never experienced the necessary repentance and faith in the One who died on a cross for them.

BY THEIR FRUITS YOU SHALL KNOW THEM

What Christian deacon or elder would run off with his pastor's wife? What leader in the church would say to his pastor: "you have driven a wedge between the two of us, and then explain in detail what a wedge is in comparison to a nail?" What influential deacon or elder would tell a pastor that his predecessor looked to him for advice on how to run the church affairs, and that he still wanted this kind of respect and attention? What group of deacons would confront a pastor about a rumor going around about him, without confronting those spreading the rumor? Why would deacons, with different views about the church, split a church in order to get their ways?

When encountering most of these leaders in speech outside the walls of the church, they tell you that they can't remember a time when they were not in church. "The church has been a part of my life ever since I was a boy," some will say. "My papa and mama dragged me out of bed on Sundays and off to church we went. I had no choice in the matter and knew what would happen if I rebelled." What Mr. Ford said in his interview with the New York Times could have been said by millions of others.

Their true love and allegiance are to the local church, and not with the Lord Jesus. They are doing what they have been doing ever since they were boys and girls. Not much has been said in the home about the Lord Jesus, for it was always about the church and the tradition of meeting there with friends and relatives.

Many of these well-respected and admired leaders sit and listen to preachers proclaim the teachings of Jesus Sunday after Sunday. They have come to believe that the minister's message is not for them, but only for others in the congregation. Their bell has never rung, sounding the need for more than church attendance. For some it has become a Sunday morning religious lifestyle and another lifestyle for the week out in the secular world.

Godly deacons, elders, and leaders are to be greatly admired by their peers, having been duly elected or elevated into playing important roles in their churches. Like in all walks of life, some go through the routine while others are indeed devoted men of God.

"UNLESS OUR RIGHTEOUSNESS EXCEEDS THAT OF THE PHARISEES"

The Pharisees were a very dedicated and self-righteous group, yet Jesus called them hypocrites. They depended on their own self-righteousness and adherence to the Law as their way into heaven. Self-righteousness and the keeping of the Sabbath will not wash away sins in a person's life and gain the forgiveness for sins that Jesus taught. Never will it be possible for a person's goodness to undo the sinfulness in one's life.

The assumption by the multitudes that churchgoing makes one a Christian is the devil's tool. Jesus said that "the road to heaven is narrow" and that "there are few that find it." The emphasis placed on church attendance, and not on Jesus, has put stumbling blocks in the roads that people are traveling today.

The apostle Paul was not only an evangelist, but taught new converts in the faith the precepts of Christianity. Some of the apostle's teachings are about his personal experience with the Lord Jesus Christ, and about the changes that were to take place in a person's life after his or her entry into the faith. It was about what God had done for him, what he had been before conversion, and what he had now become.

Paul wrote that upon acceptance of Christ, "old things will pass away" and "all things will become new." He proudly made the claim that he had died or was crucified with Christ, yet he went on living by letting Christ live his life through him. How many among the professing two-billion-plus followers of Christianity have made changes in lifestyles similar to those made by the apostle?

The apostle didn't say that everyone that repented of sins, believed, and accepted Jesus, would have the same kind of experience that he had. In his theology he didn't say converts would be "struck blind" and have an emotional experience the same as he had experienced. Paul's theology was about a change! There would be a turnaround from the way that one had lived in the past to the way that one would live in the future. This is what repentance is about—a change of direction takes place when persons become followers of Jesus. The same old roads are no longer traveled.

Are untold numbers still walking down the same roads as before? Is the lifestyle on Sunday different from the lifestyle that is being lived the rest of the week? Has there been a change of attitude and direction? Is the love for the local church more than the love for God?

The disciples that we read about in the Bible experienced a change when they had an encounter with God. Each person that comes into the kingdom of God experiences a personal encounter and a change of direction when Jesus is received. It is not about love for the church, but love for Jesus.

MEDITATION

A TRIP BACK IN TIME

My friend and I had recently read about Jesus riding into Jerusalem on a donkey, and decided that Jerusalem would be the destination on our next trip back in time.

Upon our arrival, excitement, enthusiasm, and skepticism gripped the populace. It was to be the largest week of the year for tourism in Jerusalem. People, mostly of Jewish descent, from all over the world had been arriving daily for the Passover.

Arriving in our garments of that day and time, we mingled with the crowd as we walked down dusty paths, looking at what vendors had to offer. The smiles and pleasantness displayed by vendors said that business was excellent.

On the lips of many was talk about the raising of Lazarus from the dead. "We saw it with our own eyes," one visitor to the city was saying. "Believe me, it was a miracle, and we have come here, not only for Passover, but to see what other miracles Jesus will be doing while he is here."

Walking on through the milling crowd, we saw some religious leaders whispering among themselves. The enthusiasm and excitement of the people over the arrival of Jesus riding on the back of a donkey into Jerusalem, and the raising of Lazarus, were difficult for these religious groups to play down. Their sweating brows were testimonies to their frustrations over the rising popularity among the people of the man from Galilee.

Overheard as one Pharisee talked to another, "See, this is getting us nowhere. Look how the whole world has gone after him!"

It was becoming more obvious to them that Jesus was not going away. The healings, miracles, and acts of mercy were propelling Jesus more and more into the limelight and were interfering with their teachings and beliefs. They had begun to lose respect with the people.

As my friend and I mingled, we encountered two disciples of Jesus, Philip and Andrew. A large number of people had gathered around them asking questions about their lives with Jesus, how it was to follow such a man who could work miracles, and where they would be going next. The question was asked:

"What were you doing before you followed Jesus?"

"Both of us were fishermen," volunteered Philip. "Jesus told us that we would become fishers of men. Our lives have tremendously changed, and our eyes are being opened every day to Jesus' way being our way."

There were in the crowd around Philip and Andrew some Greeks that were hanging onto each word spoken by Philip. They had come for the feast and could have been converts to Judaism.

One of them, addressing Philip, said: "Sir, we would like to see Jesus." The request of the Greeks to Philip, instead of to Andrew, could have been because Philip had a Greek name. We watched as Philip, without giving an immediate reply, went over to discuss with Andrew whether it was alright for Jesus to talk with the Gentiles. Suddenly, there was a nod from the two of them as they went off to seek an audience for the Greeks with Jesus.

My friend and I, leaving the scene, already knew that the door to God had been opened to everyone, both Jew and Gentile. Hadn't Jesus gone through Samaria when other Jews had walked around to avoid those who were half-breeds?

One person brings another, and another, and in turn, they come one by one to the Master. Hadn't Andrew brought his brother, Simon Peter, to Jesus? Everyone needs to be brought to Jesus, and not by merely introducing the local church as the way to experience God.

—derived from John 12:12-22.

CHAPTER FOURTEEN

LIFESTYLES OF SELF-PROCLAIMERS

"Do not conform any longer to the pattern of this world, but be transformed by the renewing of your mind." Romans 12:2a

LIFESTYLES CONTRARY TO JESUS' TEACHINGS

Today's culture would like to rewrite some pages of the Bible which are not in tune with current-day secular lifestyles. The Scriptures have addressed every known sin of mankind, and God has not changed. As a fallen race, humanity has missed the mark of God's intentions. If the Bible, under the inspiration of God, were rewritten today, it would remain the same as when first written. For centuries, humanity has sought the approval of God upon its sinful ways. God will forever remain the same, yesterday, today, and always.

Since God isn't changeable, humankind seeks lifestyles contrary to the teachings of God. Today's lifestyles contradict and are in conflict with God's will, since secularism promotes its own beliefs. God gives to every person a free will, which is a choice to choose His way or their way. The vast majority of people have chosen their way over God's way. Those who proclaim to be Christians, but are not, choose churchgoing as a way of penitence while living a lifestyle contrary to that of a Christian.

Culture's lifestyles permeate every institution, organization, denominational, religious, or Christian body. Nothing has remained untouched by ungodly lifestyles that have permeated the very core of every religious and denominational body since the time of Christ. The worldly lifestyles of the churchgoing masses have become the dominant force in seventy-five percent of Christian churches throughout the world. Culture's influence has been unable to rewrite the Bible, but unbelievers have succeeded in infiltrating Christian churches, especially in the United States, with their secularism.

Humankind is God's creation, made in the image of God, but became a fallen race when Adam and Eve disobeyed God. There is a void in a person's life that can only be refilled by a spiritual element upon restoration by God. Jesus says, "It is written: Man does not live on bread alone, but on every word that comes from the mouth of God." Untold numbers of churchgoing people have never had the void or emptiness in their lives spiritually reactivated by the Spirit of God.

Had our ancestors and denominational groups led those under their guidance into becoming followers of Jesus Christ, rather than placing their emphasis on churchgoing and the church building, today's practice of Christianity would be different. And if ministers had preached Jesus, instead of adapting to cultural standards and denominational doctrines, Christianity would not be experiencing the tremendous influx of the lost. If denominational greed had not pervaded and hindered the salvation of the lost, there would not be the confusion among millions as to what to believe. At fault is the absence of the practice of Christianity in the lives of the churchgoing public.

My concerns are not on judging or condemning the teachings of any particular religious group. Every person is responsible to God, who gives to everyone the opportunity to make a freewill choice. My intent is to focus on those claiming the name of Jesus whose acts are contrary to what a born-again believer should become when he or she repents of sins and accepts Jesus as Savior. Why do those who claim to be Christians live a lifestyle contrary to his teachings? The obvious answer would be that they have never repented and been converted.

The apostle Paul writing to the Church at Rome, wrote: "What then? Shall we sin because we are not under the law but under grace? By no means!"

God has relit the spiritual fuse within born-again believers. Where we were once dead in trespasses and sins, we are now spiritually born again into the family of God. Should we sin intentionally? Never! That old sinful nature still remains, and it now becomes necessary for born-again believers to stay in touch with God's Holy Spirit that is now living within them. To continue to live contrary to his teachings, and to not feel any remorse for what one does, should lead one to question one's 'spiritual experience' with the Lord Jesus. "Our spirit bears witness with His Spirit that we are children of God."

LIVING THE SAME LIFESTYLE AS BEFORE

Jane is a professing Christian who has been attending church since she was a child. When she was in her high school years, her friends were joining the church and were being baptized. Not wanting to be left out of the loop, she did the same.

After adolescence, Jane picked up new friends—some who were churched and some who were not. She was fairly regular in attendance at the local church, because that was the center for some of her social activities. During the week she displayed to her un-churched friends that her lifestyle was no different than theirs.

Jane, in her twenties, fell in love and married. But like so many marriages today, it didn't last. Luckily there were no children involved, and Jane set out on a course of partying, having what she considered her kind of fun. It became the norm to attend the "happy hours" with her girlfriends, where one could meet men, socialize, and sometimes go home with one of them.

Over the period of several years, Jane met many men, often bedding down with them for months. Sometimes these romances went almost to the altar, but men and women hang out in bars not only to drink, but to meet others who are also looking for basically the same lifestyle with little or no commitments.

"Jane," someone said to her, "if you want a person with whom you can establish a long-term relationship, you're not going to find them in a bar. Why don't you go back to church and it might be there that you meet a Christian man with whom you may fall in love?" Jane was not having any part of that, because she was not interested in going back to church except on special occasions, which were few and far between. She already knew men that went to church, but lived lifestyles contrary to their beliefs.

On one occasion she was asked by a minister if she thought that she was saved. "If you should die today, Jane, would you be in heaven tomorrow?" the minister asked.

"According to my standards or your standards?" she wanted to know.

"Let's do it by the teachings of the Bible," the minister replied.

"I feel that if I died today, that I would be in Heaven," she said.

The minister didn't pursue with Jane what her standards were, for he knew that a Christian didn't live the lifestyle that Jane had been living all of these years.

Jane continued to explain to the minister that she read her Bible almost every day, and that she had a prayer life as well. Although she was not a regular attendee at church, she was still a Christian, according to her standards.

The Bible says, "God forbid that we continue in sin. Don't you know that you are bought with a price?" And what a price! In the pages of the Holy Bible, Jesus explains to his followers: "Unless your righteousness exceeds that of the Pharisees, you will not enter into the kingdom of Heaven." How much more of an understanding is needed of what the lifestyle of a Christian is to be like?

Church rolls throughout the world have millions like Jane and just as many Johns. Some folks get 'religion' when it becomes the thing that everyone else is doing. Outside of the confines of Sunday's churchgoing, they live by the standards of the cultural world that catered to needs other than those which are spiritual.

LIVING TWO LIVES OR TWO LIES

I read with interest the syndicated column written by Jeanne Phillips, or "Dear Abby." A recent article printed the letter from a woman who had been married for nearly fifty years to "one of the best looking Christian men a woman could have." She explained to Ms. Phillips that her husband was out of the house almost every night doing church work. Everyone loved him and was always telling her that he set the best example of any man in the church.

When her husband was stricken with cancer, and had only a short time to live, he confessed to her that he had been a philandering cheat, telling her of the many affairs that he had over the years. There had been a woman in the neighborhood that had left her husband for him, and some affairs had been with women young enough to be their daughters. He was begging her not to hate him when she looked down on him in the casket.

Her husband is just a number among millions of churchgoing men and women that are living in adultery, and who are living one lifestyle in the church while engaging in another. Only unbelievers are able to continue in sin without feeling remorseful.

Surveys report that over twenty million married couples are engaged in extramarital affairs.

Only God knows a person's heart, for the Bible teaches that for the Christian who is living in sin, there will be no peace, joy, or comfort when we grieve the Holy Spirit that is living within believers. It is impossible for a born-again believer to continue year after year in sin.

The lifestyle of a Christian should not be likened to that of the Pharisees who were worshipping and obeying the Law of Moses. They believed that by the keeping of the Law, their good would outweigh the bad in their lives. But the good doesn't have the power to wash away the sinfulness in a person's life.

A Christian is the temple of the Holy Spirit that comes to live within a believer at conversion. When sins are confessed and faith and acceptance of the Lord Jesus Christ is acknowledged, forgiveness comes.

Persons who profess to be Christians, but are not, are obeying the devil and not God. A Christian has the Holy Spirit living in his life, and when straying away from the will of God, the Holy Spirit is grieved and causes the born-again believer to know that he or she is not living according to the dictates of God.

Persons who are claiming the name of Jesus, yet living according to the dictates of the devil, feel no remorse and no repentance. Day after day they continue in their sinful ways, because there is no remorse.

What is the motivation for churchgoing unbelievers, who are living like the devil's advocates, to profess knowing Jesus? The primary answer to this question can only be:

EVERYONE WANTS TO GO TO HEAVEN! They believe that God will overlook their sins if they acknowledge Him at least one day of the week.

Here in America it's still popular to claim the name of Christianity and to go to church. How long this type of popularity for Christianity will exist in America is questionable. Unbelievers infiltrating the ranks of Christianity with their lifestyles are driving lost persons outside of the church away. The Christian lifestyle is deeply rooted in obedience and love for God rather than in the desires of the flesh.

MEDITATION

A TRIP BACK IN TIME

My friend and I on one of our trips back in time encountered a group discussing a story that had just been told by Jesus to one of their colleagues. Jesus, having just left the area with his disciples, had created quite a stir within this group.

This small group of religious men had sent their smartest member to question and test Jesus about how a person could inherit eternal life.

"Did you notice?" we heard one of them say. "Jesus often comes back with a question when he is questioned about something?"

"Yes!" some answered as they agreed and nodded to one another.

One of them spoke up and said: "Jesus immediately replied to the question about eternal life by asking: 'What is written in the Law? How do you read it?' He must think that we are stupid. We've been studying the law a lot longer than a carpenter's son, and we have probably forgotten more than he will ever learn."

The man who had asked the question of Jesus replied: "Jesus knew that I knew the answer to putting God first in my life, and my neighbor next." "I should have stopped there while I was ahead. But, no, I had to test Jesus further by asking him, 'who is my neighbor?' Jesus knew that I knew who my neighbor was, and then proceeded to tell me a story about a man who had been robbed, beaten, and left for dead."

My friend and I perked up our ears, taking a few steps closer to the group, as their comments became more heated with emotion.

"What kind of ridiculous story did Jesus tell you?" asked one of the men who had just joined the group.

"Oh, he said, a man was on a trip from Jerusalem to Jericho when he was beaten, robbed, stripped of his clothes, and left half dead. Then along came a priest who ignored him by crossing on the other side of the road. A Levite soon came by and behaved just like the priest had done. Then along came a half-breed who had pity on the half-dead man, bound up his wounds and put him on his donkey, checking him in at an inn, paying for all of his expenses, and offering to pay the innkeeper more to take care of him."

"Do you believe that story could have happened?" asked someone in the group.

"Wait!" he said. "There is more to this story! Jesus then asked me 'which of these three do you think was a neighbor to the man who fell into the hands of robbers?'"

"And what did you say?" asked the man who had recently joined the group.

"You can bet your sandals that I didn't say the name of those half-breeds that we despise, for I refuse to even get close to them." My reply to Jesus was: "the one who had mercy on him." "He then told me to go and do likewise."

My friend and I saw them as they slapped their friend on the back and heard them as they laughed about the way that he had answered Jesus. The group became more boisterous as they talked among themselves.

Someone in the group said, "I don't want to be robbed and beaten, but if it should happen to me, I don't want a half-breed touching me and binding up my wounds. I would be so unclean that I couldn't even worship in the temple for days."

"Me, too," said another. "This Jesus is all wrong about who my neighbor is. If we did what Jesus wanted us to do, we would be excluded from our religious practices for our uncleanness."

"You're so right," they agreed, nodding their heads in approval. "God wants us to put him first, but surely he wants us to pick and choose our neighbors."

My friend and I walked away, shaking our heads in disbelief.

"Sounds like we're back in the States among those who pick and choose Scriptures to justify their sins," said my friend.

—derived from Luke 10:25-37.

CHAPTER FIFTEEN

A DEAD SPIRIT AND A GODLY GENE

CREATED IN THE IMAGE OF GOD

We were created in the image of God, according to what is written in the Bible. Throughout the ages, those who study the Bible have been trying to comprehend exactly what is meant by this. As humans, how do we look like God?

Looking into a mirror, I try to picture myself looking somewhat like God. Is there something in my facial expressions that resembles God in some way? Does God have eyes, ears, nose, and lips like mine? Does He have a body of flesh and blood? Sound absurd? It's a mystery to be speculated, discussed, and surmised about from here to eternity. Paul the Apostle says that we now look through a glass dimly, but one day we will be face to face.

The godly image that we bear has to be on the inside of us, and it could be in our genes. Children inherit genes from their parents, their parents' parents, and on and on we go. When we go to our physicians today, we have to tell them a complete history of family members. In treating our illnesses, physicians want to know every little detail that we are willing to disclose. So, what is wrong with every person born into this world having a godly gene?

As a mother pushed her shopping cart around the grocery store, shoppers stopped to admire and make faces at the little baby in the cart. "My, how pretty a child!" some exclaimed. He looks just like you. The mother, knowing that it might just be flattery, says, "Oh, you ought to see his father, for the baby looks exactly like him."

Another person, knowing the mother, says, "Well, Dan can't deny being the father of that baby, because the baby is the spitting image of Dan." And so it goes: the image of God has to be inside of us, and not in our physical appearances. No one can act, talk or walk like God, much less resemble God in some physical way.

The Lord God Almighty, when he said, "Let us create man in our image," was speaking, as scholars believe, to the Trinity: God the Father, Jesus Christ the Son, and God the Holy Spirit. Therefore, we must have a spiritual resemblance to our Creator in some way.

The apostle John wrote that Jesus gives "light" to every person that comes into the world. Perhaps, it's that spirit inside of us, having been put there by God when we were conceived, which bears this resemblance.

The apostle John wrote, "Dear friends, now we are children of God. And what we will be has not yet been made known. But we know that when he appears, we shall be like him, for we shall see him as he is." Undoubtedly that 'created in the image of God' is not in the physique of humankind, for flesh and blood will not inherit the kingdom of God.

THE POSSIBILITY OF A GODLY GENE

Recently, I read a magazine article that implied that "some" people might have a godly gene, while some folks don't. This "some folks don't" could be a dangerous way to look at it, because it would reveal our Heavenly Father as a God that shows favoritism. That type of thinking would cancel out many passages in the Bibles, such as "God so loved the world," or "that God is not willing that any should perish, but that all should come to repentance." Going further with this, "God is no respecter of persons" would also have to be deleted.

Perhaps God did put a godly gene in everyone, and that godly gene has been passed down from parents to children throughout all ages. When God placed Adam and Eve in the Garden of Eden, Adam was given instructions on what they could do and what their responsibilities would be. The two of them had access to everything that was in the garden except for the tree that was in the middle of the garden. Their sole responsibilities were to be obedient to God, and to tend to the garden.

The godly gene (strictly speculative) that was implanted by God in Adam and Eve at creation has now been handed down from generation to generation. Our parents passed the godly gene on to us, and we will pass or have passed it on to our children. The chain will never be broken. The children that were to follow were not to be gods, but were to become children of God. The godly gene remains the same as the one given to Adam and Eve.

Our Heavenly Father wanted to fellowship with his creation and to have a very intimate relationship with them. His desire was to walk in the cool of the Garden in sinless company with Adam and Eve, carry on a conversation with them, and to enjoy their fellowship. God's intention from the beginning was not for them to become gods, but godly. They were to be themselves and to achieve the purpose for which they had been created. This was the paradise which came before the fall of man, which happened because of their disobedience. No longer could the two of them remain in the Garden of Eden when they, through their disobedience, became sinful.

When God breathed into humanity and gave man and woman the breath of life, he gave them a free will and a spirit, and implanted within them the godly gene. The spirit that he placed inside of Adam and Eve died a spiritual death when they became disobedient, but the free will and godly gene lived on. The light of spirituality went out for the two of them when they sinned.

The spirit dies when a person sins at accountability, making it necessary for a person to be born again. Jesus in his conversation with Nicodemus had much to say about the two births. There is one birth when we are born of an earthly parent and another birth when we are spiritually reborn from above.

DISOBEDIENCE TO GOD'S WILL

From history's beginning, some have tried to become like God in attempts to establish kingdoms on earth and in the heavens. The devil and his followers were thrown out of heaven by God, because they wanted to rule. The devil is a fallen angel and because of his disobedience to God was cast out of Heaven. He continues to stage warfare between God and God's creation.

This can be reminiscent of our actions against those that are our superiors either at work or in other situations. We complain about our work situation and talk about how we would do things differently if we were in charge and had the opportunity. So were the devil's actions in his relationship with God.

It was the devil, in the disguise of a serpent, which convinced Eve that she should eat from the tree that God had forbidden. "Eat from the tree," she was coaxed, "and you will become like God." It was all a lie by the devil, who was seeking Eve's allegiance. Not only did she eat of the fruit from the forbidden tree, but she gave some to her husband to eat. It was at this moment that the two of them died spiritually. But the godly gene did not die; it went on living and was transplanted and passed down to their children. A wall of separation had been built between them and God. And just as the devil was kicked out of Heaven, so were Adam and Eve removed from the Garden of Eden.

After Adam and Eve's disobedience, God entered into the Garden to have fellowship with them. Hearing the voice of God calling out, they hid themselves from the presence of God. The two of them had become sinners, naked in their own eyes, and disobedient. They had now missed the mark of God's intentions. The devil had deceived them. Adam and Eve recognized their sinfulness, as all individuals do when they reach their age of accountability.

By trying to live two different lifestyles, today's unsaved churchgoers remain disobedient to the faith that they profess when they claim the name of Jesus. The unsaved continue to eat of the tree of secularism, while wanting to remain in the garden of Christianity. The entrance into heaven remains blocked due to their failure to repent and come by faith to the sacrifice made for them on the Cross. There remains a "dead" spirit within them that has not been reborn.

The born-again believer finds it's impossible to live two lifestyles: one at church and another while out in the secular world. A person's spirit that was extinguished upon the first act of sinning is relit upon being saved or born again. The Holy Spirit lives within the life of a born-again believer.

A Christian will not permit willful sin to continue. Adam and Eve hid from the presence of the Lord in the Garden of Eden, ashamed and embarrassed by their disobedience. A born-again believer, when sin enters, will not find peace until he or she is back to fellowshipping with the Lord Jesus.

In this country, at one time and especially among rural populations, women went around the house in their bare feet doing their chores. It is more comfortable, even today, for some men and women doing housework or other tasks not to wear any shoes or to be partially clothed.

I remember as a child when there was a knock at the door the women went running to get their shoes, putting them on before they answered the door. Sometimes the women would show more laxness if it were another woman knocking at the door. It was unthinkable for a woman not to put her shoes on if a man knocked at the door. In those days, women felt unclothed without shoes on their feet.

Adam and Eve felt unclothed when God came to the garden to have fellowship with them. They had been disobedient to God, and now, realizing their nakedness, sewed fig leaves together to hide their nakedness from God, realizing that their intimate relationship with God had been broken.

"Where are you?" God wanted to know. They tried to explain that they were afraid because they were naked. The spirituality within them had died: they had become outsiders, alienated from God, but the godly gene was still alive within them. They were ashamed, and no longer able to come into the immediate presence of God. Their fellowship with God was no longer available to them.

A FALLEN RACE AND A WAY TO ESCAPE

The spiritual aspect of Adam and Eve had been eradicated—not by something that God had done, but by their own acts of disobedience to God. The realization of their disobedience was recognized instantly by them, knowing now that they stood naked before a holy and righteous God.

The place of paradise that God had prepared for them would no longer be their habitat. They were now spiritually dead and were required by God to live outside the garden in a place that no longer would be a paradise.

We, the descendants of Adam and Eve, at birth were recipients of a God-breathed spirit, but that spirit was extinguished from our lives, as it was with Adam and Eve, when we came to the realization that we were in violation of his commandments. Some within religious circles call this realization of sin the age of accountability, which comes to everyone at various stages of life. Our God-breathed spirit dies when we first sin, but the godly gene goes on living.

God provided a way of redemption for Adam and Eve. God's declaration to the devil, in the disguise of a serpent, was "that he would put enmity between the devil and the woman and between the devil's offspring and the woman's, he (Jesus) will crush the serpent's head, and the devil would strike his (Jesus') heel." The remedy and forgiveness for sin would be provided by God through the sacrifice of His Son on a cross. A spiritual rebirth occurs for everyone who will acknowledge Jesus Christ as Savior and accepts God's grace in repentance.

Adam and Eve didn't need the Ten Commandments that God gave to Moses to know that they were sinners. These commandments came years after Adam and Eve and were to provide for all generations a guide to make them knowledgeable about what God expected from his Creation. These commandments became a mirror that would point out to everyone their sinfulness.

The Law is explicit in pointing out humankind's relationship to God and their neighbors. The one thing that the Law does not provide, however, is a remedy for our sinfulness. No matter how hard a person may try to keep the Law, there is no solution or relief from sin afforded by the Law, once the Law has been transgressed, except through Jesus. When the spirit that God puts in us is extinguished upon sinning, it can only be lighted again when a person, through repentance and faith, allows Jesus into their lives.

Jesus told Nicodemus that he (Nicodemus) must be born again. That is called the spiritual birth. God does it all for us. Even though we have been disobedient and sinful, God provided the sacrifice and atonement for our sins when Jesus was crucified on the Cross. God provides for not only our spiritual needs, but our physical needs as well. He "made garments of skin for Adam and his wife and clothed them."

There are no perfect people, and every person is in need of the spiritual birth. The spirit within everyone that died when first sinning has to be relit, and that only happens when sinners repent of their sinfulness, acknowledging that Jesus is the sacrifice for their sinfulness. Only through God and His Grace (Jesus) can that spirit be reactivated.

Some might have questions about the spirit that died within us when we became sinners. How then, it might be asked, can a newborn baby have that spirit, if the parents have never been spiritually reborn? The spirit of a person does not come from the parent, but from God. It is God that gives us breath.

This is understandable when we read the Scriptures and the writings of John: "Jesus is the true light that gives light to every person. . ." A newborn not only inherits the godly gene passed on by his parents, but the God-given Spirit passed on by the One who is the Light of the World.

MEDITATION

A TRIP BACK IN TIME

My friend and I continued our walk around Jerusalem trying to gain firsthand information from eyewitnesses about recent happenings. Many were milling around in a festive atmosphere permeated by the coming observance of the Passover feast. Some Jewish boys from outlying regions, being required to be here after becoming twelve, stayed close to their families. Young and old, walking the paths and shops together, were greeting old friends, as well as strangers to the city.

My friend and I had not seen the first placard. There were no open denunciations by the Jews against their captors, nor was there overt dissent among religious parties. Overtly, it was the busiest of times, mostly among males, trudging up and down these dusty paths with their greetings. Covertly, within some of these groups, as evidenced by their whisperings and unhappiness, agendas and vendettas were being planned.

The name of Jesus was on the tongues of those who had been there when he rode into the city on the back of a donkey. Most everyone knew where Jesus could be found, for by day he would be at the temple teaching. It was rumored that by night, he would go to Bethany to stay with Simon the Leper or off to some secluded place to pray and be alone.

Some disciples that had followed Jesus into the city were talking about a woman who had poured an expensive jar of alabaster on the head of Jesus at the home of Simon the Leper. His disciples had considered her generosity to be wasteful, only to hear Jesus say that she had prepared his body for burial.

My friend and I spotted Peter and John undoubtedly hurrying to meet a man carrying a jar full of water. He would lead them to a house where they would say to the owner: "The Teacher asks where is the guest room where I (he) may eat the Passover with my disciples?" Peter and John would then be shown a large upper room where they were instructed to make preparation for the meal.

Over at the temple, the Pharisees and Sadducees were going, at separate times, to Jesus with questions in their attempts to trap him. Their efforts were becoming more frequent now, and no matter how desperate they became — Jesus' popularity with the people continued. Those hearing Jesus' teachings were amazed at his authority.

The more questions the Pharisees and Sadducees asked of Jesus, the more these religious leaders' authority and popularity eroded with the people. There had to be an opportunity for them to arrest Jesus away from the crowd and to kill him.

Judas Iscariot, one of Jesus' disciples over in another part of the city, went off with a question to the chief priests: "What are you willing to give me if I hand him over to you?"

They counted out for Judas thirty silver coins. With the clinking of each coin, was Judas hearing the words of Jesus, "you cannot serve both God and Money?"

The groundwork for the arrest of Jesus had been laid. Humankind's religiosity would soon be knocking at the palace of Pilate. A decision about what to do with Jesus had already been made by some of the most God-fearing, law-worshiping men of that time.

Future generations would not question others about who knew what, when, and where. Instead, the question asked by Pilate to the crowd that had gathered outside his palace would be echoed and asked of humankind around the world throughout the ages: "What shall I do, then, with Jesus who is called Christ?"

— derived from Matthew 26, 27; Mark 14; and Luke 22

CHAPTER SIXTEEN

PREACHERS, CHURCHES, AND CALLINGS

PREACHERS: GOD-CALLED OR A CHOSEN VOCATION

S ome preachers would like to say, "give me an audience and I'll preach to them." I have never known a preacher that loved preaching to empty pews. And I have known only a few preachers who are willing to knock on the doors of the lost. Many prefer staying within the confines of the church and not out among the people.

A vast majority of ministers are serving churches where, within their own membership rolls, the fields are white for harvest. Some are well aware of the lost that are within their own congregations, but won't confront the obvious, because the larger the congregation, the greater are the financial gains.

Most ministers of the gospel of Jesus Christ would like to believe, and have others believe, that their calling to preach is a call of God. Some will readily say that it isn't of their choosing to be a minister, but that their calling is similar to the calling of the prophets and chosen men of Biblical times.

Some ministers like to talk about what they gave up in order to answer the call of God to become preachers. Most ministers, therefore, will testify to the very end that they are God-called instruments.

God's calling doesn't hold true, however, for every minister that stands in the pulpit preaching, "thus says the Lord." Some have chosen religion as their vocation or career, and some have been recruited by religious bodies. Choosing the ministry as a vocation often comes after encouragement from parents, relatives, secular and religious teachers, and some denominational recruiting. Very few, if any, of those who have chosen the ministry as their vocation, will admit to their "choosing" instead of God's "calling."

Some ministers in today's pulpits are lost and without Christ. Their actions and deeds are testimonies to this statement. Undoubtedly, there are those who are there for varied reasons. One would conclude that if preachers were truly called by God, they would be saved and true believers. For that reason, the majority of preachers will say that they are God called, and if not God called, they would not be in the ministry. There is the desire on the part of all ministers to erase any doubt from anyone's mind that they are not a God-called preacher.

It shouldn't be too surprising or shocking to believe that in today's society there are ministers in pulpits in every denomination who are not called or saved. There were false prophets and teachers in Biblical days. They willingly told the people what they wanted to hear. Some ministers today are simply a carry-over from the pages of the past.

A minister in Florida who had been on a particular field for over twenty years stood before his congregation on a Wednesday night to confess an affair that he had been having for years with a member of the congregation. A minister in Georgia commits suicide after it was discovered that he was having sex with young boys. Scandals come out of the closets of every denomination; within the Catholic Church; in non-affiliated churches; in the Praise the Lord ministry; and in many other religious groups.

We have only to pick up a daily newspaper, watch the television, and get on the internet to hear about the demise of some evangelist or minister. It's only the well-known that we mostly hear about; therefore, we don't hear about the less known where it happens with frequency.

Are these, who have stood before their parishioners for years preaching the Gospel, saved and called of God? Only the Almighty has the answers. I can offer only an opinion as to their spiritual condition. Some men of the cloth glory in the title of "Reverend," placing clerical decals on their vehicles, and seeking the praise of others.

No one should seek a double standard for men and women of the cloth, but everyone should be asking for godly men and women who are willing to seek God's will for their lives. Unsaved and saved church members wouldn't remain comfortable in the pews if they were under the preaching of Godly men and women of the cloth.

With such an infiltration of unsaved members in churches where as many as seven out of ten church members are possibly lost, some of these lost souls have to be a reflection on preachers, and their leadership. It is evident that even God-called ministers, in their quest for members, are enticing the unsaved to add their names to church rolls without introducing them to Jesus Christ.

The major and minor prophets of Old Testament times were Godly men, but their preaching was ignored by the masses. These prophets were not trying to build membership and sanctuaries to suit the deacons, elders, or influential members. Their proclamations were to turn people back from their disobedience to God. During Old Testament days, hearts were hardened and ears were deafened to the call for repentance and obedience to God. The Old Testament prophets remained faithful in preaching God's message.

CHURCHES: SMALL AND LARGE

Many churches are experiencing a declining membership, while some churches are bursting at the seams. Megachurches are popping up all over the world, necessitating the need for larger churches and family centers to be built. Thus becomes the need for a larger staff and a minister for every imaginable age group.

On the other hand, there are churches, especially those in smaller communities, where the membership has become aged, people have moved away, and doors are being closed. The Sunday night service has become a thing of the past, and revivals are unheard of throughout many denominations. Programs and advertising are only some of the methods being used to bring the outside world in.

The larger churches are trying to become a 'one-stop' service for every imaginable need of humankind. And some are merely meeting only the physical needs instead of the spiritual needs of the person.

The larger the church, the easier it is to find a place to get lost and to avoid responsibilities. There are tens of millions across these United States who come only for the "pause that refreshes" that is being offered during the worship hour. This could be all that some churchgoers want, and is all the time that most are willing to give of their time.

It is the belief of some denominations and religious bodies that in order to gain members, the church has to add activities that are being offered in the secular realm. Arguments are offered as justification by saying that such programs are ways to reach people for Jesus. However, if these attractions are being offered by churches, where unbelievers outweigh believers, are secular activities going to take on a spiritual significance?

One does not have to leave the confines of some mega-churches to find fast foods being sold to those who have come with physical appetites. It is required by some churches, that in order to participate in some of the extracurricular activities such as athletics, one has to be a member of the church. Some, because of this prerequisite, claim the name of Jesus in order to participate.

Programs and activities offer a wonderful opportunity to present Jesus to all participants, provided the recipient is there primary for spiritual enrichment, and that it is being offered. Some come to participate only in activities other than spiritual ones. Many programs deliver only the physical aspects with a tacked-on spiritual element.

It is reminiscent of a rescue mission, where those coming off of the streets for a night's lodging and a meal have to participate in a worship service before the other amenities are afforded. These down-and-outers adapt to the prerequisites in order to survive. They participate in the spiritual rites in order to satisfy their physical needs. All participants hear the Word of God before their physical needs have been met.

PREACHERS: THEIR CALL OR ASSIGNMENT TO CHURCHES

There are denominational or church requirements for ministers or religious workers which have to be adhered to by those seeking a call or an assignment to a church. The standards set by religious bodies and denominations can vary.

When a person feels God is calling him or her into full-time service, it is customary to talk first with the professional staff at the local church. Usually this is done with the pastor or a member of his staff. Questions will be asked, prayers offered, and recommendations made. Persons who believe that they are being called into a religious vocation will usually present themselves to the church for their blessing, prayers, and approval. Those who are being called will often enter learning institutions to prepare for Christian service. Some churches will license a person to preach before ordaining them to the ministry.

In some denominations, ministers are assigned to churches by officials within that body. Pastors are moved annually by these officials or will be approved to remain in their local setting. Congregations can recommend the removal or retention of their pastors to authorities within their denomination. The decision remains with these denominational leaders as to whether a pastor is reassigned or will remain.

The majority of Baptist churches are autonomous or independent bodies. They are affiliated with conferences and conventions, but remain independent entities. Each church is responsible for calling their minister, which is usually done by the recommendation of a pulpit committee appointed by church members.

When a Baptist church is without a minister, the pulpit committee receives recommendations from others, and will venture out to other churches to hear other preachers. The pulpit committee will eventually invite someone to come to the church for a trial sermon. The local congregation, after hearing a trial sermon by the prospective pastor, will, upon the pulpit committee's recommendation, vote for or against the prospect. Interim pastors, in most cases, will fill pulpits until a minister is called.

It is considered unethical for a Baptist minister, whether now serving a church or without a pastorate, to submit a resume to a church. Some go around to the back door and have friends or relatives put their hat into the ring. It is much more difficult for a Baptist minister to find a church than it would be if he were affiliated with a denominational group which assigns ministers.

Regardless of the ways that churches choose or call their ministers, politics will always play a role. I have known of Baptist ministers that have offered their pulpits to ministers for their use when seeking a call, only to have them in turn submit their names as a candidate to the pulpit committee. A pulpit committee usually will have their own requirements for selection, whether scriptural or not.

Standing before you in pulpits across the world are ministers who are called by God, and ministers who have chosen the ministry as a profession. In physical appearance, there is no way of knowing whether the minister is a professional in the common sense of the word or whether the minister is God's chosen instrument. Ministers are to be chosen by churches by following the leadership of the Holy Spirit, and after the prayers of the people.

There are many dedicated ministers preaching in pulpits across America. Their hearts are into serving the Lord. They weep with hearts that are heavy for those who are lost. They go prayerfully out into the fields and highways, knock on doors, ministering to those whom they have been called to serve. When persons don't walk the aisles after their sermons on Sunday, they pick up their Bibles and continue with their ministry for the lost. They are doing what God called them to do, for they know that only God gives the increase.

MEDITATION

A TRIP BACK IN TIME

My friend and I had chosen to remain 'back in time,' having been fascinated by the conversations that we were hearing about Jesus. Since arriving in Jerusalem, there were speculations galore, and we were hearing from those around the city that strange and climatic happenings were in the making. No one bothered to explain what might happen when or at all during Passover, when people from all over had come to the city.

"I can feel it in these old bones of mine," said an elderly, bearded, gentleman. "I have been around Jerusalem all my life, and these developing events are like none other that I have ever known. Our religious leaders are consistently meeting and talking about Jesus, and his being here. They are saying that he is possessed by demons. Everywhere he goes, they follow, trying to trap him by his teachings. Their leadership is being questioned, and they fear that a revolution against our conquerors will follow unless Jesus is quieted."

"You are so right," said one of his companions. "You know what some are saying about Jesus: that he is a prophet or the Messiah. Well, I have been reading the scrolls, and in those scrolls there is talk about a Messiah. Zechariah, the prophet, wrote something about our King coming to us riding on a donkey. Could Jesus be the promised One?"

"I can answer that question for you," said another person from the group. "If Jesus was the Messiah, he wouldn't have ridden here on a donkey. Can you imagine Jesus stirring up a revolution on a donkey? A great white stallion would have been the choice of the Messiah!"

"That's for certain," said the elderly bearded gentleman. "He would have come with a flaming sword to drive away our conquerors. God promised us a Messiah, and God keeps His promises. No one should question that Jesus is a religious man, and sent by God. Could anyone do the things that Jesus has been doing unless God be with him?"

"We've heard what Jesus did at the temple," another one of the men added. "They say he went into the temple, turning over tables and benches, and not allowing anyone to carry merchandise through the temple courts. He told those that he was teaching that 'my house will be called a house of prayer for all nations.'"

"With this kind of zeal for the 'house of the Lord,' perhaps he is the Messiah," someone from the group added.

"Whether Jesus is the Messiah or not, said another, it was time that someone did some cleaning over at the temple, because it was difficult to feel God when there."

My friend and I turned and walked away from the group, wondering what Jesus would do if he dropped in on most of the churches in America.

—derived from Mark 11:15-18.

CHAPTER SEVENTEEN

HELL: THE DESTINATION OF UNBELIEVERS

God doesn't send anyone to hell. It is a choice totally made by the unsaved. Hell is an eternal place for those who have not repented of their sins and have not received the Lord Jesus as their Savior. It's true that our Creator is a loving God, and that he doesn't send anyone to hell. With our free will, we make the choice. God's creation chooses and makes life's decisions, and one of the decisions made before death is where to spend eternity.

Hell is:

> The absence of God
> The absence of love
> The absence of joy
> The absence of peace
> The absence of kindness
> The absence of patience
> The absence of choice
> The absence of self-control
> The absence of hope

The absence of forgiveness
The absence of mercy
The absence of goodness
The absence of compassion
The absence of light
The absence of water
The absence of coolness
The absence of freedom
The absence of blessings
The absence of salvation
The absence of space
The absence of loved ones that choose heaven over hell
The presence of eternal fire

LIFE ON EARTH IS NOT A HELL

There will always be those who believe that they are now living their hell here on earth. After death, there is no recourse for the decisions that were previously made while in the body. According to the Bible, after dying a physical death, there is a vast chasm existing between the living and the dead. No number of candles that are lighted or prayers offered for the departed will be able to obtain a transfer to another abode. What right does the living have in making a decision for a person who, while living, preferred a life apart from God?

In a movie named "To Hell and Back," the starring role was played by Audie Murphy, the most decorated soldier in World War II. Mr. Murphy believed and felt that he had been to hell and back, for war is awful. Mr. Murphy had been in the thick of many battles and had returned. Circumstances that he experienced involved more than those without battle-field experience could imagine. His experiences were to him a hell here on earth. Mr. Murphy lived through awful situations and was able to return to normalcy where there was the absence of warring conflicts. The hell that Jesus speaks about, however, is a place from which no one will be able to return.

Contrary to what some may believe, the Holy Bible does not speak of a place where departed souls or spirits go to await their final destination. There are many who believe that the dead can be prayed out of a place called purgatory by friends or relatives that are still living. Candles are sold and lit for the departed and prayers are offered to the Almighty. The Bible doesn't teach that someone can make a decision for another. Our final destination is determined by us, and by no one else.

If there were the existence of such a place as purgatory, would these departed ones that were there, want someone to pray for their deliverance? I would think that there could be only one answer to such a question. Surely, with the descriptive awfulness that Jesus spoke about hell, an opportunity to escape the portals of hell would be readily acceptable. These departed souls, however, chose their destiny when here on earth.

LAZARUS AND THE RICH MAN

Jesus didn't talk about purgatory, but he and his followers did teach about hell and its horrors. "The time came when the beggar died and the angels carried him to Abraham's side. The rich man also died and was buried. In hell, where he (the rich man) was in torment, he looked up and saw Abraham far away, with Lazarus by his side. So he called to him, 'Father Abraham, have pity on me and send Lazarus to dip the tip of his finger in water and cool my tongue, because I am in agony in this fire.' But Abraham replied, 'Son, remember that in your lifetime you received your good things, while Lazarus received bad things, but now he is comforted here and you are in agony. And besides all this, between us and you a great chasm has been fixed, so that those who want to go from here to you cannot, nor can anyone cross over from there to us.'"

The rich man wanted Abraham to let Lazarus go and warn his five brothers so that they would not end up with the same fate. Abraham assured the rich man that his brothers had Moses and the Prophets to listen to. However, the rich man believed that if someone from the dead came and told them about the place that he was in, that his brothers would listen to them. Abraham's answer was that if they didn't listen to Moses and the Prophets, then they wouldn't listen if someone from the dead (Jesus) were resurrected.

The parables that Jesus told were contrasted with everyday truths and happenings. We encounter, walk in, through, and around those that Jesus talked about in his teaching parables. Around the cross were gathered sinful men similar to the lost five brothers of the rich man in the parable. When Jesus was crucified, dead, buried, and raised from the dead, had they believed? There are millions of unbelievers sitting in church pews today with beliefs and unbelief running through their heads, but not in their hearts.

HELL: AN EXISTENCE WITHOUT GOD

When we speak or use the word "hell," it is associated with the worst possible thing. Some people, in their anger, tell others to go there. In the Old Testament, "Sheol," or the grave, which was believed to be under the earth, was the place of the departed dead. The word that is used for "Sheol" in the New Testament is "Hades," the realm of the dead. Jesus' parable is about the rich man being in Hades and about Lazarus being in heaven with Abraham.

Near Jerusalem was the valley of Hinnom where children were sacrificed to pagan gods. Gehenna or hell was named after this valley and New Testament writers refer to this as being the place prepared for the devil, his angels, and unbelievers. This was the place or a place similar to this, the final and eternal state of these after the resurrection and the last judgment.

Some people have concluded that there is no such place as hell. Some form this opinion because it is seldom preached anymore. When was the last time that you heard a sermon on hell and its consequences? Jesus didn't hold back in his teachings about hell and alerted those that would listen, that hell awaited those who were not repentant by their turning to the Living God.

Some are of the opinion that God is merciful, gracious, forgiving, and good, and that their sins are not awful enough to warrant them ending up in hell. There is no question here about the attributes of God. What has been forgotten is that God cannot condone sin, and that sin has its punishment.

Mark, the gospel writer, quotes Jesus as saying, "If your hand causes you to sin, cut it off. It is better for you to enter life maimed than with two hands to go into hell, where the fire never goes out. And if your foot causes you to sin, cut it off. It is better for you to enter life crippled than to have two feet and be thrown into hell. And if your eye causes you to sin, pluck it out. It is better for you to enter the kingdom of God with one eye than to have two eyes and be thrown into hell, where 'their worm does not die, and the fire is not quenched.'"

Preachers aren't preaching about hell today because it is offensive to the ears of unbelievers in their congregations. Some ministers will openly admit that they don't feel comfortable preaching about hell. I wonder how Jesus felt about his preaching of the subject. It was compassion and His love for the sinner that compelled him to warn about the danger of ending up in hell.

Many preachers stay away from subjects that are offensive to the ears of their congregations. Ministers are aware that their parishioners want to leave the confines of the church feeling good about themselves and their way of life. Christianity is in the flourishing throes of secularism, and so are many who pound on pulpits today.

The time that the apostle Paul spoke to Timothy about is here and has been here for a long time: "For the time will come when men will not put up with sound doctrine. Instead, to suit their own desires, they will gather around them a great number of teachers to say what their itching ears want to hear. They will turn their ears away from the truth and turn aside to myths."

MEDITATION

A TRIP BACK IN TIME

There was to be no death row wait for Jesus, nor would there be an appeal made on his behalf. He was made to carry his own cross to Golgotha, and after he became too weak to bear the weight, Simon from Cyrene was forced to carry it.

Jesus, with a criminal on each side, was nailed to his cross, then lifted up by the soldiers and set in place. Jesus' cross, being in the center, enabled the two thieves to have equal access to Jesus. It's amazing how God works in our lives, providing everyone the opportunity to have access to Him.

My friend and I heard one of the criminals hurling insults at Jesus as he turned toward Jesus and said: "Aren't you the Christ? Save yourself and us!"

My friend and I understood perfectly what the criminal was asking. It was all about his wanting to physically come down from the cross and to return to his way of life. He had not looked into the future and was only living for today.

Instantly, the other criminal came to the defense of Jesus. "Don't you fear God," he said, "since you are under the same sentence? We are being punished justly, for we are getting what our deeds deserve. But this man, nodding toward Jesus, has done nothing wrong." Then, turning his head again toward Jesus, he said: "Jesus, remember me when you come into your kingdom."

My friend and I recognized the repentance flowing through the words of the other criminal. It was not about today, but about tomorrow.

"I tell you the truth," said Jesus, "today you will be with me in paradise."

There was no recognizable remorse nor were there to be any further insults from the other criminal.

My thoughts continued to digest the words that came from the deathbeds of these two criminals. One of the two had come to a saving knowledge of Jesus, and would be in heaven today, and the other one was on his way to hell.

It was about three o'clock in the afternoon when we heard Jesus cry out again from the Cross, "My God, my God, why have you forsaken me?"

Some standing around the cross thought that Jesus was calling out for Elijah. Again, Jesus cried out in a loud voice, and gave up his humanity.

My friend turned to me and asked: "was this the cup that Jesus didn't want to drink, his being separated from God when he took on the sins of the entire world?"

"You're right," I responded. "God cannot condone sin, and had to depart from it. Sin separates us from God, and Jesus has done for us what we couldn't do for ourselves."

Fear and darkness began to envelope us as the earth shook, rocks split, tombs and graves were being opened. It was at this moment, we would later learn, that the curtain in the temple was torn from top to bottom. All people could now come directly to God by way of the Cross. No longer would one have to go through a priest or a holy man to obtain access to God.

Most of the onlookers, some beating their breasts, began drifting away. We watched as some of Jesus' followers continued to stand at a distance.

It was then, off in the distance, that we heard a voice cry out: "Surely this man was the Son of God."

I turned to my friend to say, "There is another believer who will see Jesus in heaven one day."

"How sad for some of the others," he said. "Almost everyone here today went away without saying: 'Jesus, remember me when you come into your kingdom.'"

—derived from the gospel writers.

CHAPTER EIGHTEEN

THE HEAVENLY HOME

"In my Father's house are many rooms; if it was not so, I would have told you.I am going there to prepare a place for you." John 14:2

EVERYONE WANTS TO GO TO HEAVEN

For the born-again believer, it doesn't take a rocket scientist to figure out for them if there is a heaven and a hell. It's all about faith. All humanity wants heaven to be their final destination, and prefers heaven over an eternity in hell. Speculations and summations about heaven and hell can be drawn from any and all quarters of the globe. For born-again believers in Christ, how, who, and when entry into heaven is possible are drawn from the pages of the Bible and what Jesus had to say about the subject.

The Word of God teaches that the only way to enter heaven is repentance, faith, acceptance, and the receiving of Jesus as Savior. There should be no confusion about that! The speculations and confusions rest with those who, having never read or studied the Bible, believe that there are many ways or roads that will lead them there. Not everyone believes that Jesus is the gate or entrance to heaven, for there are other religions and beliefs.

In an Associated Press article, Jeffrey Burton Russell, an emeritus professor of history at the University of California-Santa Barbara, is quoted as saying, along with others, that "the way Christians in the United States conceive of both heaven and hell is so feeble and vague that it's almost vague 'superstition.'" "It's not that heaven is deteriorating," he says. "But we are." "Some people are so confused they believe in heaven but not God," says Russell.

In the same article, questions were raised as to who would enter heaven. The article quotes a Newsweek/beliefnet.com poll last year that asked, "Can a good person who isn't of your religious faith go to heaven or attain salvation?" Seventy-nine percent said yes, with somewhat lower percentages among evangelicals and non-Christians.

It was reported in the same Associated Press article that the Second Vatican Council (1962-65) declared that people who do not know the Christian gospel but sincerely seek God "can attain to everlasting salvation." The Catholic Church decided that requiring explicit Christian faith was too pessimistic, said U. S. theologian Cardinal Avery Dulles, writing in First Things magazine.

A Gallup poll in 2004 reported that eighty-one percent of Americans believed in heaven and seventy percent in hell. An earlier Gallup sampling said seventy-seven percent of Americans rated their odds of making heaven as "good" or "excellent."

But now, Cardinal Dulles cautioned: "Thoughtless optimism is the more prevalent error. Many Christians mistakenly assume that 'everyone, or practically everyone, must be saved.' Christians are permitted to 'hope that very many, if not all, will be saved.' Still, the New Testament teaches 'the absolute necessity of faith for salvation' and says that each of us faces just two possibilities, either 'everlasting happiness in the presence of God' or 'everlasting torment in the absence of God.'"

There is no "council" or "declaration" that can change or falsify the teachings of the Bible. Jesus explicitly declared that the way to enter heaven was "through him" and through the "spiritual rebirth" of each individual. In order to appease the masses, some denominations have modified the teachings of Jesus to conform to the wishes of their followers.

How many churchgoing folk will enter the Pearly Gates of heaven? No one here on earth knows the answer to that question. For a certainty, churchgoing, opinions, declarations, and councils, are not ways or roads to heaven. It can only be speculated, surveyed, researched, and talked about. Multitudes, whether Christians or not, are interested in talking, reading, or hearing about heaven, and how to get there.

UNTOLD MILLIONS ARE ON THE WRONG ROAD TO HEAVEN

Ask those that you come in contact with daily if they are going to heaven when they die. "I hope so!" will be the answer by many of those who are quizzed. Some might even say, "I think so!" Some will say that they are living by the golden rule, while some are wishing and hoping. Few answers with certainty about getting there are offered by persons being polled about heaven.

Why is there so much doubt among so many as to the way to heaven? Heaven, among many, has become a denominational and personal philosophy that doesn't come from the Bible. Born-again believers are looking beyond the grave with the expectation that to be "absent from the body is to be present with the Lord" who is seated at the right hand of God, the Father. The location of heaven is where Jesus went to prepare a place for born-again believers.

In a nation where the Bible is very popular and available, but perhaps scantily read, you would believe that a church-going public would know the way to heaven. Are the persons of the cloth teaching the Bible with expository preaching that removes the doubts and give to listeners the pathway to those Golden Gates? A few ministers might be doing that, but a vast majority of preachers are not. When was the last time that you heard a sermon about heaven? Could it have been at someone's eulogy when the mourners were being given assurance that the departed person was now with God?

We have been led to believe that the United States has a large number of Christians. Researchers say that seventy-seven percent of the population of the United States falls into three religious groups: mainline Protestants, evangelical Protestants, and Catholics.

There are millions who call themselves Christians throughout many denominations and various churches. Those who say they are Christians are varied in their beliefs. Their actions don't testify to their claim of Christianity—only their tongues. Not even an adequate definition of Christianity can be given by those proclaiming their Christianity.

Being the possessor of a Bible, having a belief in God, living in the United States, and going to church aren't the qualifiers for entry into heaven. Bibles have been translated from earlier manuscripts, and some of the present-day translations have been printed in easy-to-read English. There is no reason for a reader to remain in a state of doubt or frustration about life beyond the grave. The truth is that the Bible is being neither read nor preached. Even after reading the Bible, many will question its authenticity.

Within the pages of the New Testament are the teachings of Jesus about heaven. Jesus said things about heaven to those that came into the hearing range of his voice. His hearers were told how to get there. For the readers of the Bible, there should not remain any mystery on how to enter the place prepared for Jesus' followers. The spirit that died at sinning has to be rekindled by the light of Jesus.

Paul, the apostle, was taken up into the third heaven by God to receive a glimpse of what was to come after his physical death. Paul afterward writes that he "heard inexpressible things, things that man is not permitted to tell." To keep Paul from becoming conceited about these 'surpassingly great revelations,' he "was given a thorn in his flesh, a messenger of Satan, to torment him." Paul paid a tremendous price for his visit to the third heaven, but not comparable to the price that Jesus paid on the cross in getting every born-again believer to paradise.

Recently I went with another minister to visit a lady who is dying of cancer. The minister, wanting to read some from the Bible, asked the lady if there were a Bible nearby. "There's one here somewhere," she replied. What we do with the Bible is similar to what some do with other books that they purchase—lay them aside, unread, forgetting where they have been put.

JESUS IS THE ROAD TO HEAVEN

"I am the way and the truth and the life. No one comes to the Father except through me," says Jesus. There is only one way to interpret this verse, because it goes directly to the heart of the matter and is not contradictory to any other passages from the Bible. It is so simple that even a child can understand its meaning. That is how God wanted it to be.

I remember seeing a western movie where the good guys were up against a larger number of bad guys. One of the good guys was sick and dying, and his partners had to find a friendly home where the sick one could rest and regain his strength. When it came time for them to leave, the companions of the sick man had to leave their sick friend with their host, because he was not well enough to travel. He assured

177

them that their sick friend would be safe with him. "Don't worry," he said. "If they (the bad guys) come after your friend, they will have to come through me." Basically, this is what Jesus is saying to everyone: "Those wanting to reach Heaven will have to come through me."

There was an interesting article in Readers Digest entitled "In Search Of Heaven," written by Gail Cameron Wescott. The article begins by saying that Barbara Walters "interviews true believers to find answers." At first glance, I surmised this to mean that everyone that Ms. Walters interviewed was a 'true believer' of Christianity. However, should her statement also be interpreted to mean that those interviewed were true believers in God, true believers in Heaven, or true believers in their own religion? My understanding of this article led me to conclude that the ones interviewed were 'true believers' in their respective religions, but left me still questioning Ms. Walters' definition of "true believers."

The article further stated: "There are some 10,000 religions in the world, and nearly all incorporate teachings of an afterlife. In America, nine out of ten people believe that heaven is a real place—and most have faith that they are going there at the end of their lives." This article puts the number of Christians in the world at 2.1 billion people.

People are living in a fantasy world of "hoping, wishing, and believing" that they are going to end up in heaven. Some folks have fantastic dreams of winning the lottery, visiting foreign lands, owning planes and boats and having all the money that they could ever spend, but for most, these dreams will never be realized. Hard-earned dollars are plunked-down, chances are taken on getting rich, but at the end of the day, millions go home with empty pockets and diminished dreams. At death, where will these "true believers" spend eternity?

Pews are full of churchgoers who are "hoping, wishing, and believing" that they will end up in heaven. And Jesus is saying to everyone, "you have got to come through me." Jesus says, "Enter through the narrow gate. For wide is the gate and broad is the road that leads to destruction, and many enter through it. But small is the gate and narrow the road that leads to life and only a few find it." At the end of a lifetime, untold millions will have taken the wrong road.

THE ROAD TO HEAVEN IS NARROW

All of us have traveled down roads and highways. Traveling down some of the paved two-lane, fifty-five-miles-per-hour highways in America, I find that some are narrow, curvy, and not very well maintained. Unless I'm interested in seeing some Americana, I barely can wait to get back onto the interstate highways where established speed limits are being exceeded in getting to a planned destination.

Riding down some narrow two-lane roads in Indonesia some years ago, I remember how I could have touched hands with those in approaching vehicles when they passed by. It was frightening having to experience an approaching truck with blaring horns claiming more of the road than the automobile I was traveling in. It was not a pleasant experience. Jesus did say that the road to Heaven was a narrow one, and we need to be able to reach out and "touch" Him while traveling the highways of life.

God looked into the future and saw what future roadways and highways his creation would be traveling. The building of these interstates makes it possible for the populace to zoom, when traffic is right, mechanically down these thoroughfares, enabling humankind to reach their human destinations. Although these thoroughfares are crowded, wide and speedy, millions will not be exiting at the one road that leads to heaven.

Churchgoing, goodness, the absence of Biblical preaching, and the many non-biblical beliefs on how to get to heaven, are similar to broad highways heading in the direction of a place up ahead called "destruction." The traffic jams that will be encountered along the way are like reminders of the many times that God's message was heard, but never heeded. Only born-again believers in the Lord Jesus Christ will be able to overcome the roadblocks and traffic jams, because they have received their directions from Jesus.

Jesus told the parable of the ten bridesmaids: "At that time the kingdom of heaven will be like ten virgins who took their lamps and went out to meet the bridegroom. Five of them were foolish and five were wise. The foolish ones took their lamps but did not take any oil with them. The wise, however, took oil in jars along with their lamps. The bridegroom was a long time in coming, and they all became drowsy and fell asleep."

"At midnight the cry rang out: 'Here's the bridegroom! Come out to meet him!'"

"'Then all the virgins woke up and trimmed their lamps. The foolish ones said to the wise, Give us some of your oil; our lamps are going out.'"

"'No,' they replied. 'There may not be enough for both us and you. Instead, go to those who sell oil and buy some for yourselves.'"

"But while they were on their way to buy the oil, the bridegroom arrived. The virgins who were ready went in with him to the wedding banquet. And the door was shut. Later the others also came. 'Sir! Sir!' they said. 'Open the door for us!'"

"But he replied, 'I tell you the truth. I don't know you.' Therefore keep watch, because you do not know the day or the hour."

Jesus in his parable about the ten virgins could have been telling a parable about ten churchgoers. However, five out of ten from today's churchgoing public being ready for his coming might be a tad too high, for seven out of ten churchgoers today appear to be unwise. Five of the ten virgins were ready when he came back to earth, and five of them were not.

Jesus' specific instructions are to be ready when he returns. It will be too late when death overtakes a person or when Jesus comes back to claim the redeemed. "I don't know you," are his words to those who have been playing church.

There were ten lepers that met Jesus on one of his trips to Jerusalem. In a loud voice they called out to Jesus to have pity on them. Jesus commanded that they show themselves to the priests. As the men went to carry out the orders of Jesus, they were cleansed of their leprosy. Only one of them, a Samaritan, came back to throw himself at the feet of Jesus and to give thanks for his healing. Jesus asked, "Were not all ten cleansed? Where are the other nine? Was no one found to return and give praise to God except this foreigner?" Then he said to him, "Rise and go; your faith has made you well."

Out of the ten that were cleansed only one came back to thank Jesus. The other nine went back to what they were doing before being isolated by their leprosy. Many who start out following Jesus, whether in the church, through baptism, with their lips, or with an intellectual acknowledgment, never have followed him with their hearts. In this parable recorded by Luke, it is noted that out of ten people, only one became a true follower of the Lord. Seventy-five percent or more of the churches in America will remain almost full should the Rapture occur today.

Jesus says, "For I tell you that unless your righteousness surpasses that of the Pharisees and the teachers of the law, you will certainly not enter the kingdom of heaven." Christian righteousness is intended to be lived from the inside out, not from the outside in. The quality of our life is to be displayed differently from that of the Pharisees, a very religious group, during the days of Jesus. The Pharisees were keepers of the law and by their outward appearance, displayed their religiosity. Christians, with the Holy Spirit's indwelling, enables God to work his righteousness through them.

Members of the churchgoing public who are without Jesus as Savior are merely spectators and speculators waiting with the wrong ticket stamped "churchgoer" in their hands. Somewhere in life, they failed to get the ticket that was printed in blood and signed by God. There will not be another act to follow the Cross. Nor will there be an intermission. Heaven awaits only born-again believers who are saved by God's grace.

MEDITATION

A TRIP BACK IN TIME

It was early morning in Jerusalem, and surrounding the Roman governor's palace, a large crowd had begun to gather. Back home in America, Christians would be celebrating this day as Good Friday. In many areas of the world, bells from church towers would be chiming tunes of hope. For multitudes, this would be celebrated as a holiday whether one believed or not in its significance. Holidays are like rain and sunshine, falling on the unrighteous as well as the righteous.

It was not to be a peaceful day here in Jerusalem, for daybreak brought with its arrival accusations against a man who claimed that he was God.

My friend and I had lingered in Jerusalem to get a better understanding of why the happenings of this day would come to be called by so many people "Good Friday." As we approached the palace of the Roman governor, people were gathering to see what was taking place.

Only moments before, Jesus had been bound and led to the palace by a party of high-ranking Jewish religious leaders. Reaching the grounds of the palace, they turned him over to the Romans. His accusers knew that if they went inside the palace, they would become unclean, and therefore would not be able to participate in the religious ceremonies planned for that week. By no means were they going to become unclean by entering the residence of a pagan. They would now stand and wait in the courtyard for Pilate to come out to them to hear their accusations.

My friend and I watched as Pilate, the Roman governor, came out of his palace to ask of the man's accusers: "What charges are you bringing against this man?"

"If he were not a criminal," they replied, "we would not have handed him over to you."

"Take him yourselves and judge him by your own law," Pilate said.

"But we have no right to execute anyone," the Jewish leaders interjected.

The purpose and intent of their bringing Jesus to Pilate was now made known. Nothing but a death sentence for Jesus would appease the accusers.

My friend and I watched as Pilate, several times, went back into his palace to talk with Jesus, and then back outside to address the crowd. It had become a tedious time for Pilate because there was not enough evidence against Jesus to support the charges that were being made. Pilate had considered the advice given by his wife, and also had heard from Herod, the ruler of Galilee. The decision to set Jesus free or to sentence him to death was Pilate's to make. After an exhausting morning for Pilate, it became decision time.

We listened as Pilate asked the crowd, "What shall I do, then, with the one you call the king of the Jews?"

"Crucify him!" they shouted. The frenzy of the crowd became more intense as others in the courtyard began to take up the chant of "crucify him."

My friend and I were beginning to get caught up in the emotional and fanatical mood of the crowd. Our lips moved and our voices, too, wanted to call out the words to "crucify him." At that moment we became aware of our sins, and it was for our sins that he was going to die. My friend and I were also guilty of crucifying Him. Jesus was going to die in our place, providing instead of punishment, our reconciliation with God.

As we watched, Pilate took some water and washed his hands in front of the crowd. "I am innocent of this man's blood," he said. It is your responsibility!"

Upon hearing this from Pilate, all the people answered, "Let his blood be on us and our children!"

I turned to my friend and said, "It is by His blood that we are cleansed. Thank God for this blood cleansing that will be offered to everyone who believes."

"Yes," he said. "Jesus paid it all!" "We can wash our hands in water like Pilate while trying to become clean, but only Jesus' blood can cleanse us of our sins."

"All of us are guilty of crucifying Jesus," I said. "We are just as guilty as his accusers who brought Jesus to Pilate. It is because of my sins and the sins of the world that He was crucified."

The pounding of the nails into Jesus' hands and legs would soon be replaced by church bells around the world on Good Friday chiming notes of "forgiveness, peace, joy, hope, and love."

My friend and I were there, and also responsible, the day they crucified our Lord.

—derived from Matthew, Mark, Luke, and John.

CONCLUSION

My purpose for this book has been to bring an awareness of what is being practiced, believed, and lived by those who claim the name "Christian." Engaging in churchgoing activities for untold millions of churchgoers has become only a habitual tradition. Churches and churchgoing don't make Christians, for God alone can do that.

Every person on this earth who believes that there is a God, wants to go to a place called heaven when they die. The price tag for going there is not paid for by our attending church services. Jesus paid the price for our sins, not churchgoing.

I am reminded of the two young incarcerated men, who, after hearing the gospel message, asked me to save them. With all the compassion that could be mustered, I answered: "I can't save you; only God can save you." We prayed together and they asked God to forgive their sins, and to save them. They had a heartfelt need and a repentant heart for forgiveness of their sins, and went to the only One who was able to save them.

What is being practiced and lived by the vast majority of churchgoers today is not Christianity. If these printed pages will cause anyone to examine their relationship with the Lord Jesus and come to repentance and faith, these pages will not have been in vain.

The apostle Paul writing to Christians in the church at Corinth said: "Examine yourselves to see whether you are in the faith; test yourselves. Do you not realize that Christ Jesus is in you—unless, of course, you fail the test?"

An old farmer prowling the booths one morning in a fast food restaurant asked a young man, "Whose son are you?" In essence, he was asking who his parents were, and was checking to see if there was any resemblance. The world is waiting for the image of God to be reflected in today's Christianity. After conversion, the saved become sons and daughters of God, and are adopted into His family. The behavior of today's churchgoer gives testimony to the world as to whom we belong.

Churchgoers either belong to God or to the devil. Allegiance is devoted to one or the other, and lifestyles are testimonies either for one or the other. It is impossible for any one to live for Jesus only one day of the week, while living for the devil the other six days. The Holy Spirit living in each born-again believer will not tolerate the continuation of a sinful life.

Employers seek complete dedication from employees by wanting their loyalty. It would be highly inconsistent, immoral, and unethical for employees to promote the work or the products of competitors. That is what happens when the unsaved claim the name of Christianity, but whose life-styles are contrary to such claims.

Churchgoing, manmade programs, preachers, confirmations, baptisms, living a good life, or any other human element, will never make anyone a Christian. Salvation comes as a yielding act of the will of an individual to the will of the Heavenly Father. Churches can lead people to Jesus, but can't make them drink of the life-giving water of salvation.

As children, we sought justification for everything that went wrong in our lives and grew accustomed to blaming others for mistakes. We answered to our parents for our mistakes, while desperately attempting to appear guilt-free of any wrongdoing.

Around homes there were playhouses, tree houses, toys, and pets where children were able to live out their fantasies. These things became escape mechanisms where make-believe friends were met. Becoming comfortable in such settings, minds dreamed of faraway places where make-believe dreams and ambitions became real.

Adolescent days eventually came to an end when maturity set in. Other avenues and venues took shape. Toys were put away, having been replaced by other interests that, hopefully, would bring some degree of peace and solitude. Mama and Papa no longer were there to heap praise, bind up bleeding hearts, and to give encouragement. The apostle Paul writes: "When I was a child, I talked like a child, I thought like a child, I reasoned like a child. When I became a man, I put childish ways behind me."

Leaving the nest, other means and methods were soon sought to fill the existing void. Many, having grown up in the church, became aware of their sinful ways, repented and received Christ, and were saved. Others left the church and began to drift away with the feeling that since they had been introduced to Christianity, that they were now Christians.

Then, there were the others who also grew up in the church, believing that just attending church was all the salve they needed to heal their sinful ways. Instead of God filling the void within the lives of children who had grown up in the church—the church, instead of Jesus, became what some people came to believe was their salvation.

You can't take the unsaved out of the church, and it's difficult to take the belief of being a Christian away from the unsaved. The belief that attending and being a member of the church meant being saved was implanted long ago. Parental teachings were implanted during childhood days, but were mostly about churchgoing attendance. Multitudes are holding to the belief that because of their upbringing by Christian parents, they are Christians.

The watered-down version of today's Christianity will not bring the churchgoing public to their knees. When rain is sent down from heaven to water the earth, it has to be the tears of our Lord over the way that the unsaved churchgoing public is abusing his Name.

Using the New International Version of the Bible, several passages have been quoted in this book without identifying where they might be found. I have intentionally failed to give Biblical references in the hope that the reader will make a diligent search to prove their validity, and to further read from the pages of God's Word.

Meditations were added to the ends of chapters so that reader's minds could recapture the events that did happen thousands of years ago. Jesus did suffer, did die, was buried, and did rise from the dead. He did it for everyone's sins— past, present, and future. Jesus, instead of the church, is humanity's way back to God.

My prayer for every reader is that he or she puts their trust in the One that died for them, and not in churchgoing, church membership, good deeds, or some false teaching.

So you want to go to heaven? Churchgoing won't get you there.

To God be the glory, great things He has done through our Lord Jesus Christ.

Printed in the United States
201964BV00001B/319-366/P